USER-DEFINED SOFTWARE

USER-ORIENTED SOFTWARE

DEVELOPMENT AND DELIVERY

A COMPLIMENT TO AGILITY

and

PRODUCT LINES

HOFF INDUSTRIES

DEDICATION

User-Defined Software writers dedicate this document to those who participate in developing software and made a sacrifice for its development to deliver a quality capability for the user.

To all my Air Force friends I have known throughout my Air Force career, both as an Officer and Civil Servant. The forty-five years I have served have enabled many people to cross my path.

To my children Tara, LeAnn, Amanda and Maegan, and their children Cameron, Deana, Chadrick, Maverick, Brodrick, Jaymee, and Olivia and Chris Davidson and Chad Svenby, my son-in-law's.

To all friends and family who I have known throughout my life.

Table of Contents

ACKNOWLEDGEMENT

To Dennis Notareschi, a trusted patriot, who provided a key element in this document centered from his quotation. When I asked, "What does software represent?" Dennis provided a lasting and most influential statement, "Software is a representation of the real world upon which it was built."

To Dave Kissane who helped expand Dennis' statement, with an additional thought on software. "Software, therefore, also represents and includes product delivery for users' needs such as events, function, process, and objects all transformed into digitized matter, both those known and not yet discovered."[1]

[1] Frederick Hoff, "Software Workshop," Spring 2013.

CHAPTER 1 – INTRODUCTION

USER-DEFINED SOFTWARE (UDS) MODEL

UDS origin dates to 2003 where it was successfully introduced in the development of software as a process different from the traditional Waterfall Model outlined in Annex D. The UDS model provides for the delivery of capabilities with both speed and quality, along with a cost-effective solution. UDS is very much in-tune with leading frameworks in industry with one fundamental difference – UDS focuses on delivery of a product for the user of the capability.

USER-DEFINED SOFTWARE

The UDS model is more than a <u>framework</u> for software development, but also a <u>methodology</u> for a cohesive and collaborative environment to deliver a capability based on the needs of the user. UDS model links to a 1995 Integrated DEFinition Model (IDEF)[2] workshop to model Supply System of the Future. During the workshop, expert Air Force Supply resources were brought together from throughout the Air Force to identify the process and determine where improvements in the future system could occur. IDEF is a modeling technique and identifies Inputs, Controls, Outputs, and Mechanism (ICOMs)[3] along with improvement opportunities. These experts were Users and not the Customer.

However, emerging frameworks at the turn of the 21st Century were using the term customer throughout their models. Later in 2005 the foundations of the UDS model emerged labeled as the 4-D's: Determine the Requirements with the Customer, Determine the Design with the Customer, and Develop with the Customer and Deliver with the Customer. (See Annex D for a depiction of the 4-D's model) The key element of the 4-D's was the elimination of an elaborate requirements and design documentation process. It was then realized Customers were Users of the software. Developers and Users met two times a week to collaborate and discuss coding progress and identify next development needs. These meetings took a label called 2 A-Week Meetings. The software developed using the 4-D's is still in production today, nearly 20 years later and has served the Air Force efficiently.

Within industry the Agile[4], Spiral, Incremental, Scrum[5], and other developmental

---

[2] "IDEF Family of Methods, A Structured Approach to Enterprise Modeling & Analysis", IDEF, http://www.idef.com/
[3] Ibid.
[4] Kent Beck, et al, "Manifesto for Agile Software Development", 2001, https://agilemanifesto.org/

frameworks and methodologies emerged with an emphasis on the customer.[6]

"Scrum is a process framework that has been used to manage work on complex products since the early 1990s. Scrum is not a process, technique, or definitive method. Rather, it is a framework within which you can employ various processes and techniques."[7]

Also, taking a seat in software development is the visual model called Kanban[8], which originated at Toyota to improve manufacturing processes. Kanban is a combination of two Japanese words: 'Kan' for visual and 'Ban' for Card. The key for Kanban in software development is the ability for visual tracking the process and progress of schedule work for bugs, defects, new work etc.[9]

The 4-D's model took on several names such as Customer Focused Software and Software by the Numbers, but it wasn't until recently that the need for a complete revamping of the 4-D's framework emerged which lead to User-Defined Software model. UDS as compared to other frameworks is based on *USER* involvement and their input throughout the delivery of the capability, regardless if it is for software maintenance or a new system or anything under development.

UDS recognizes and appreciates other software frameworks, development methodologies and modeling techniques. However, these frameworks and

---

[5] Ken Schwaber and Jeff Sutherland, "The Scrum Guide™", November 2017.

[6] "12 BEST SOFTWARE DEVELOPMENT METHODOLOGIES WITH PROS AND CONS", Acodez, June 01, 2018, https://acodez.in/12-best-software-development-methodologies-pros-cons/

[7] Ken Schwaber and Jeff Sutherland, "The Scrum Guide™", November 2017, p3.

[8] David J. Anderson, "Kanban: Successfully Evolutionary Change for your Technology Business", 2010, https://www.digite.com/kanban/what-is-kanban/

[9] "The Ultimate Guide to Kanban Software Development", kanbanize, https://kanbanize.com/kanban-resources/case-studies/kanban-for-software-development-teams/

models work at a high level of abstractions, which limits their explanations of necessary details to adequately develop software.

UDS is a ***user-oriented software*** development <u>framework and methodology</u>.

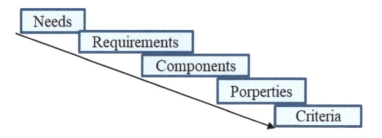

Figure 1.0-UDS Initial Steps

UDS incorporates short iterations and increments development activities, and like other frameworks focuses on a quality, user acceptable product over a time-box delivery. The model demonstrates user acceptance throughout the work. High user involvement reduces risk of a rejected product by the users at the time of delivery.

The UDS processes show that a single increment or multiple increments may be released into production. The goal of the UDS process is working software, which is in concert with the Agile Manifesto[10].

UDS <u>does not favor extensive upfront documentation</u>. It does favor an extensive Test Plan as the critical documentation. An example for a Test Plan is in Annex A. The Test Plan can serve as the primary document for preparing other documents at the end of the project. The Test Plan will capture all the needed

---

[10]Kent Beck, et al, "Manifesto for Agile Software Development", 2001, https://agilemanifesto.org/

artifacts for a requirement specification and user design document. Database experts can likewise derive database specification from the test scripts in the Test Plan. The actual database Entity Relation Diagram (ERD) is a specialized document prepared by the database experts and is needed for visualization of the database.

Historic development frameworks and methods had long documentation upfront work, which delayed delivery of the capability. Throughout software development history, Senior level managers, functional and front-line user advocate for quality software. However, the lack of ample test professionals drives a poor delivery of quality in the products. UDS supports the need for test professional both those who perform the test and those software developers who build and maintain the test environments. The need for software test professionals is the missing link in quality software.

Today, other software development procedural frameworks have the goal of delivering quality software under cost with frequent releases.

UDS combines processes and proven methodologies for the delivery of quality products on-time, without extensive cost overruns. The key to success is adaptation.

CHAPTER 2 - CRITICAL REASONING FOR INFORMATION TECHNOLOGY (CRIT)

By using CRIT, the UDS team will be able to decompose the user needs into Components/Requirements/Properties/Criteria and Complexities with sufficient confidence to move the need through the UDS model.

"What is Critical Thinking? The intellectually disciplined process of actively and skillfully conceptualizing, applying, analyzing, synthesizing, and evaluating information gathered from or generated by, observation, experience, reflection, reasoning, or communication, as a guide to belief and action.

USER-DEFINED SOFTWARE

In its exemplary form, it is based on universal intellectual values that transcend subject matter divisions: clarity, accuracy, precision, consistency, relevance, sound evidence, good reasons, depth, breadth, and fairness."[11]

So how does CRIT enable an Information Technology solution should be a stark question at hand? It structures the team to think beyond the inherent current visuals of the problem. CRIT compels the team to <u>reason through the needs</u> to derive solutions and requires the application of a body of knowledge found only in seasoned professionals, who can enhance their understanding of the needs by skillful dissecting the problem into its parts.

CRIT enables the UDS team, including IT professionals, to gleam the purpose, and create the vision of the end state. CRIT helps establish a clear understanding of the <u>need at hand</u> where software can envelop the results based on the concept of Critical Thinking. CRIT allows the team to explore all environmental and technical factors (such as security, performance, timelines, etc.) which affect the delivery of the capability to meet the need.
CRIT utilizes a series of questions:

> ➤ Who is it for,
> ➤ When is it needed,
> ➤ Where is it to be used,
> ➤ How will it be used,
> ➤ What are the expected outcomes?

---

[11] Defined by the National Council for Excellence in Critical Thinking, 1987, A statement by Michael Scriven & Richard Paul, presented at the 8th Annual International Conference on Critical Thinking and Education Reform, Summer- 987.

USER-DEFINED SOFTWARE

By continuously asking and answering these questions, the professionals are then able to formulate assumptions and establish reasonable expectations from various alternatives to achieve the desired results.

CRIT fosters a federated family of highly skilled professionals such as functional analysts, architects, engineers, database experts, cost and economic analysts, and contractual and legal minds to work the need. Front-Line User, Functional User, Corporate User and the originator of the need are main members in the UDS team as the capability evolves producing result responsive to the original intent.

CRIT, in its epic state, forms the foundation for the UDS model, because users tend to think in terms of needs, actions, and solving problems. Everyone thinks in, and along these lines, however, the order of what and why users think is dynamic. The demand for better software development and delivery methods within industry and governments have challenged the historic rules associated with software discipline.

As part of CRIT evaluation the UDS team must address:

> ➤ Volatility to ensure stability,
> ➤ Complexity to ensure proper time/level of skills for the project,
> ➤ Ambiguity to remove the possible misinterpretation,
> ➤ Uncertainty to reduce the risk of producing a wrong or unusable product.

The goal of CRIT is to provide a means to reason through the need and formulate the necessary logical purposes for why the creation of an Information Technology capability should become a reality.

Before we depart this portion of UDS, it is necessary to gain an understanding of the scientific laws of information. According to Dr. Gitt, information is non-material, and thus, he declares it to be massless. It originates through will; it can be changed, gained, and lost.[12] This single position about information makes it uniformly different than material matter.[13]

Understanding the UDS model is extremely important. Because through CRIT expanding the body of knowledge, regarding information, is the process of gaining knowledge (will) of the individual or team of individuals to comprehend the knowledge in the form of information. The body of knowledge, therefore, consists of what is known. However, as the knowledge expands, then what is known likewise expands. CRIT's design is to make anyone grow their own body of information. Expansion; of what is known; is possible through understanding the realities, truths, and detecting the intrinsic characteristic by fact-finding through questioning and seeking answers. Until answers are formulated and proven, the whole of the knowledge surrounding the information is lacking.

Using CRIT, anyone can expand their own body of knowledge and information (both are non-material). Last, a person can draw a correct conclusion about information and knowledge as it exists today. Information and knowledge are present everywhere, throughout the universe. Our universe of knowledge contains what we know. Therefore, what we don't know is undefined; because the expansion of the body of

---

[12] Werner Gitt, "Scientific laws of information and their implications—part 1; Extracted from the Journal of Creation-23 (2) 96—102, August 2009, https://creation.com/laws-of-information-1
[13] Ibid

knowledge has not yet obtained the information.

CHAPTER 3 - UDS TEAM

The team for the UDS Model must be all-inclusive. The actual hands-on users of the product are foremost the most critical aspect of the development process.

UDS team(s) composition

User (Front-Line, Functional and Corporate) *
    Software Developers*
    Systems Engineers*
    Database Experts*
    Technical Writers*
    UDS Facilitator*
    Test Developer*
    UDS Lead*
The team members listed above, with the asterisk (*), are part of the cohesive team, who work together daily to deliver the capability.

The number of teams is dependent on the size and complexity of the needs and the total scope of the needed capability.

The list of members below contains occasional members who are participants as needed to ensure the product is meeting the expectation of the needs.

> Acceptance Members,
> Capability Owner,
> Implementation Planner,
> Product Owner,
> Test Manager.

(Note: For an expanded definition for new terms, please refer to definitions in Annex F at the end of the document.)

Team Cohesion

When addressing cohesion, team location is dependent on the scope of the effort. Does the team have to be collocated in the same environment? The answer has many variables. Before the enhanced communications; we have today; the answer would have been affirmative. However, today, the need for colocation is not necessarily the case. One caveat to this statement is the need for a new system. Throughout UDS development, team meetings in the development environment for collaboration is highly recommended.

If the need is for maintenance of a capability for a product running the field, then the colocation of the entire team is not necessarily needed. However, experience has shown having the maintenance developers and skilled functional users, those who are familiar with the capability, collocated; is beneficial in terms of an immediate response to the software changes to meet expectations.

CHAPTER 4 - DETERMINE USER NEEDS

CUSTOMER VERSUS USER

Before diving into the process of determining user needs, it is essential to gain an appreciation of the actual user. Far too often in any project attention is focused on the top official or senior person within the organization. They tend to drive the needs, since they are often considered the key person. They have always been considered the person with the money, the decision-maker, the authority, and therefore, the most important. However, having them considered the most important person in the construction and development process is a major mistake and a flaw. Let's settle in on a few fundamental definitions at this junction because they will be used repeatedly in the remainder of this document.

What is the difference between a customer and a user? It is critical to make and draw a clear distinction between these two terms. Quite often in the realm of information technology, the word customer is a misused term, which has misguided software development in general. In business, is a customer a person who enters a place of business? The answer is NO because until the person makes a purchase, they are what is typically called foot traffic, lookers, prospective buyer, or someone who is cost comparing. In truth, these people are prospects and only become customers when making a purchase. A customer, therefore, is a buyer, patron, and even a client in other professions.

Likewise, in software development, it is correct to consider the customer as the payer for services. The higher authority who is in the position to make the contract or obligation to complete the work. Rarely will the customer equal or have the level of responsibilities as a user. A user, on the other hand, is the heart of the software effort and the primary purpose of the software. The software must be developed for the user of the product and not focus on what the customer or higher-level authority dictates. If the senior authority is directing the development without the end-user, then the development becomes a senior corporate level structured development with a stovepipe, single-minded approach. The end-user, in many instances, will not be happy with the product and will often reject the product. Throughout the UDS model there are major deviations from other models. There is no start and stop end dates but a continuous process of development, using daily *analysis* to achieve the results. Analysis is not contained in a process step as an independent activity, but

<u>analysis is continuous</u> throughout the UDS model from the original needs' assessment to the delivery. Even after delivery of the capability an analysis is accomplished to assess the user satisfaction.

From a pure sense of the word, Merriam Webster defines "need" as: a situation in which someone or something must do or have something; something that a person must have; something that is necessary in order to live or succeed or be happy; a strong feeling that you must have or do something. Webster's full definition is:

1 - Necessary duty or obligation;

 2(a) - A lack of something requisite, desirable, or useful;

 2(b) - A physiological or psychological requirement for the well-being;

 3 - A condition requiring supply or relief;

 4 - Lack of the means of subsistence or poverty.

For our purpose NEEDS in the UDS MODEL aligns with Webster's definition 1, 2(a) and 3 with tangible results.

ORIGINATION OF NEEDS

For the development of software, a fundamental understanding of where the needs for software development originate.

An essential aspect for this portion of the UDS model is to keep in mind FIRST Level Needs and avoid the deep dive into the details of the requirements. There are 3 conduits for needs see Figure 4.0 below:

USER-DEFINED SOFTWARE

Figure 4.0 Origins of Needs

ENTERPRISE NEEDS

These needs vary but are considered those tools used throughout the industry, such as those needed for network-related connectivity. When these or other tools become unstable/outdated, or the vendor introduces a new product that disables version support, typically the result is an enterprise related upgrade. Enterprise technical enhancements span across all echelons software systems and contain varying degrees of changes. Technological changes create enterprise needs. The enterprise assessment is, therefore, directly related to these technical changes. Additional consideration about technology is the newness of the technology and its readiness for commercialization or use within the industry or government. Newer, untested or unproven technology brings risk. Also, these enterprise needs could drive a maintenance activity to an existing system as detailed below.

USER-DEFINED SOFTWARE

NEW CAPABILITY NEEDS:

> Needs generated from an assessment for a totally new capability. From a functional perspective, a common way to think of these new capabilities as a downward directed need. The typical process begins with a functional community with a need, and they then analyze existing systems' capabilities. If the analysis determines the existing systems do not have the needed ability, then, the results is a need for a new capability. Like in Enterprise needs assessment, adding a new capability will most often generate a series of enhancement/maintenance needs in other parts of adjoining systems. In the new capability analysis, additional hardware, manufacturing processes, etc. could all play a significant role in the assessment. With the need for new technology identified in this assessment, it is system-specific and not enterprise related. A classic example of a system-specific new capability within the banking industry was the addition of the ATM card. The purpose and use of the ATM technology point to system-specific capability and not an enterprise need.

EXISTING SYSTEM NEEDS:

> *ENHANCEMENTS:* Within this subcategory, a need exists for enhancements to an existing capability currently in use resulting from a process or procedural changes. Process/procedural or functional changes are part of the assessment within existing systems. But on the other hand, it is not good enough to accept, 'we have always done it that way." Referring to the ATM card discussed previously, as a new capability; the banking industry and general businesses went through many software enhancement iterations to

enable the use of the ATM card for customer purchases versus the use of a credit card.

> *MAINTENANCE:* "There are four types of maintenance, namely, corrective, adaptive, perfective, and preventive. Corrective maintenance is concerned with fixing errors that are observed when the software is in use. Adaptive maintenance is concerned with the change in the software that takes place to make the software adaptable to new environment such as to run the software on a new operating system. Perfective maintenance is concerned with the change in the software that occurs while adding new functionalities in the software. Preventive maintenance involves implementing changes to prevent the occurrence of errors."[14] In the life cycles of software, significant incidents for the repair of defects, historically, have occurred immediately following the release of the software. However, over time, the software stabilizes, and the maintenance actions shift from repair (Corrective) into the other areas mainly to make functional changes (Perfective). Please note software maintenance in one area of a system quite often drives a shift in another portion of the system or even subsystems.

> *REFACTORING:* Refactoring is another form of software maintenance where the software becomes unstable due to many factors, such as change or turn over in personnel, design flaws, code that is performing poorly. This leads to a need to rewrite the code commonly referred to refactoring (Preventive). It is not incorrect to lump this work under maintenance, but

---

[14] Dinesh Thakur, Types of Software Maintenance, ECOMUTER NOTES, http://ecomputernotes.com/software-engineering/types-of-software-maintenance .

refactoring is such a significant endeavor that keeping it as a separate

subcategory is appropriate because the entire system changes.

(NOTE: From a strategic military perspective an assessment of the threat also brings needs necessary for countermeasures against the threats. It is not the intention of this document to detail the strategic process in detail. However, the process does occur to maintain military superiority, which assures peace of mind. Assessing the strategic threat within the military perspective as a countermeasure generates needs.)

USER NEEDS ASSESSMENT

Continuing with the Origination of Needs within the New Capability and

Existing System Needs the most critical element is to focus on the user. In Figure

4.1 below notice the constant reference to the 'user.'

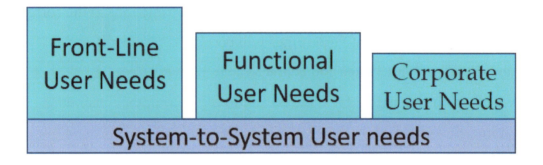

Figure 4.1 User Needs Assessment

> *FRONT-LINE USER:* Analyzing the front-line user is foremost the heart of
> the need's assessment portion of the UDS model. Gathering front line user's
> needs begins with discussing and talking with them along with other key
> element or leaders in the work center. Front-line users, predominantly
> consumers of the information, are those who use the system daily in the
> performance of their job. Front-line users range from the factory production
> line, office staff, etc. A front-line user is anyone with hands-on use of the

software capability or is considered the receiver of the information generated by the software. Front-line users can also include section chiefs or a line chief in an assembly line. Their needs must have a balanced assessment. However, it is essential to note the needs assessment must begin in the work center.

➢ *FUNCTIONAL USER:* Far too often, the development of software systems happens with the wrong people dictating the system's needs or the flow of a system. Not only is it important to capture the hands-on needs in the assessment, but also to gain a functional understanding from the functions performed in the work center. The key in the functional analysis is to group the workers' needs into buckets. The functional analysis requires talented and skilled functional resources to ensure placing the functions in the correct buckets or groupings. These groupings will become components of the systems laced with attributes and characteristics of the system. A knowledgeable and skilled facilitator is key to the decomposition and grouping.

➢ *SENIOR CORPORATE USERS:* The needs of senior corporate user can't be overlooked. These users will garner and depend on the metrics of the organization in terms of viability to maintain production and financial solvency. Spending time gathering the needs at the corporate level has an impact on the front-line and functional users because corporate use of their data is keen for decisions.

USER-DEFINED SOFTWARE

➤ *SYSTEM-to-SYSTEM INTERFACE USERS:* The word interface, in this case, is not the user screen, which by all rights is an interface, but the interface is considered another system performing additional logic. Most frequently, the Interface User has a specific defined format for the data, which has to be gathered and laid out such that the UDS development team can meet the Interface User Needs. Interface User Needs can come from all three of the major users per Figure 4.1 above.

In the next diagram, Figure 4.2, please observe Front-Line User identifies the majority of needs. While this is very important, the UDS model considers ALL users. The figure below encapsulates the above discussion depicting the volume of needs and where to focus the efforts to gather the needs.

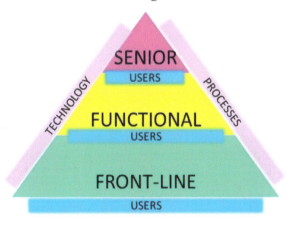

Figure 4.2 User Needs Diagram

Also note the technology and processes drive needs throughout all three of these user's levels. Technology and process side bars affect the users in the model. System-to-System Interface Users are considered separate users.

Before concluding this portion of the discussion, the reader should group and establish priorities for needs. The grouping is part of the team's responsibility to identify the most critical work to be accomplished first. One rule to ensure success in the development, especially for new capabilities is to achieve the most complicated portion of the effort early in the development. Typically, this should be done first, because the complexity could result in changes to previously developed software. If working with a new team, a recommendation to accomplish the complex portions once the team has formed and gone through typical teaming composition.

Development of user needs statement of expectation is typically done away from the work center. However, the UDS team must visit the work center to gain a full appreciation for the use of the software. These visits are crucial to garnering the processes and procedures.

STATEMENT OF EXPECTATION

Expectations span across the entire UDS model and vary depending on the work effort. From an existing system perspective, such as maintenance, the expectation is reasonably straightforward to ensure the UDS team accomplishes the repair on-time with a quality product. The burden of meeting expectations belongs to the Project or Program lead for managing the work effort. The UDS model does not 'time-box' the software maintenance delivery but focuses on quality products to meet expectations of the need. Time to deliver a product is also important, but the quality has more value. If by chance, the team cannot meet expectations, then leadership will have to intercede.

USER-DEFINED SOFTWARE

VISION STATEMENT

For a New Capability or a Major Enhancement, post generating the need, a VISION STATEMENT is critical to kick off the effort and establish the basic ground rules for the work effort. The VISION STATEMENT is the instrument used to define the strategic purpose and goals, and to establish the basic ground rules for the work effort. The VISION STATEMENT can assign a structure for the accomplishment of the work, as well as identify expected funding needs. Entities such as the government and the military have specific guidelines to follow for work efforts that exceed certain funding thresholds, and these guidelines require adherence. Likewise, corporate entities will have their unique guidelines.

The VISION STATEMENT in the form of Program/Project Management Directive (PMD) authorizes the effort. PMD is the first formal correspondence for the project and serves to meet any audit requirement and assign essential duties and roles. The PMD is not a lengthy document but a concise letter with an optional attachment for establishing roles. After signing the PMD, then the UDS model focuses more on the delivery of the capability and less on documentation. For more information on preparing a Vision Statement refer to the Product Line-Chapter 11.

CHAPTER 5 - DEFINING NEW CAPABILITY REQUIREMENTS

DETERMINING THE SET OF REQUIREMENTS

A fundamental flaw in the history of software development was a lengthy requirement process to capture and document the requirements. The documentation and process followed the Waterfall Methodology (see Annex D). However, the needs for the capability typically vanished or was overcome by newer needs, before the software was delivered.

USER-DEFINED SOFTWARE

Even more troublesome, the requirements were rarely captured along the lines of a user, as explained in Chapter 4. Times are changing with demands for timely, accurate, and cost-effective software.

In new capability software development activities, once the Needs are determined, generating the requirements is next in the UDS model.

WHERE DO REQUIREMENTS ORIGINATE?

➤ **First** - requirements will come from users' needs from their knowledge of processes and procedures, problems in the work center, observations, visual acuity. Requirements in this area are considered Critical. These requirements are preceded with the action verbs 'shall or will.'

➤ **Second** - requirements are generated from Wants and Desires (WD). Often these items are not included in the initial fielding of the need but typically are part of a subsequent software release. If the product team can accomplish some of the WD, then adding them is at the discretion of the leadership assuming there is enough funding. The combination of First and Second-Order Requirements form the main requirements. (Note: Critical, Wants and Desires (CWD): **C**ritical equals must-have needs, **W**ants equals moderate needs and **D**esires equals would like to have.)

➤ **Third** – 'I want it when I see it,' requirements are generated from uncertainty and unknowns. Unfortunately, this is the worst-case scenario because the actual end state isn't exactly known. Users often draw or sketch their ideas, and conclude by saying, "This is kind of what I want." Regardless, in this case, there is enough visual acuity to generate a requirement. What is known is only partially complete; however, enough exists to create the idea, a model or prototype often will fill the void during the development.

WORK BREAKDOWN STRUCTURE (WBS)

The portion of the UDS model within this section draws upon the excellent definition of a WBS provided by Jennifer Bridges, "deliverable-oriented hierarchical decomposition that offers digestible tasks for team members to meet the project's objectives and create the required deliverables."[15]
The UDS model depends on a UDS team working together to create a capability to meet the needs. The technique within the UDS model deviates from the traditional software development methodologies where the total decomposition occurs before the coding work begins. UDS is counter to historic, lengthy documentation development customs based on establishing comprehensive upfront specification and plans, which change throughout the project. Needs are generated throughout the UDS model and began with a need's assessment described earlier.

To get the WBS accomplished, recall the UDS team works together to accomplish the decomposition. The technique to accomplish the WBS is best accomplished near the work center. The team needs to make frequent visits to the work center to get the needs from specific users.

---

[15] Jennifer Bridges, What Is a Work Breakdown Structure? Project Manager, June 3, 2014, https://www.projectmanager.com/training/what-is-a-work-breakdown-structure

USER-DEFINED SOFTWARE

Within the decomposition activities a few visual tools are needed for the work.

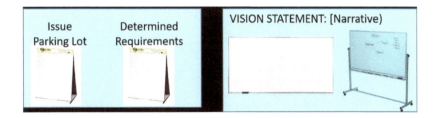

Team cohesion between the facilitator and the UDS team is crucial in the activities needed to continue with decomposition. The UDS facilitator or team lead needs to use visuals tools for the process. The Kanban[16] method is excellent for capturing and tracking ideas. A technical writer and an automated tool are also extremely important.

DECOMPOSITION

NEW CAPABILITY WBS

Below in Figure 5.0 is a repeatable WBS model for a new capability. The steps in this model are not intended to be extensive but accomplished quickly to move into development rapidly. The success is dependent on the UDS team's understanding, and once there is enough information the software developers, including database expert, can begin the development process. Getting to that stage in the UDS model is the intention of the UDS WBS. Secondly, success is also dependent on an understanding; nothing is firm at the beginning of the UDS

---

[16] David J. Anderson, "Kanban: Successfully Evolutionary Change for your Technology Business", 2010,, https://www.digite.com/kanban/what-is-kanban/

model.   Use the Statement of Expectation and/or the Vision Statement described in Chapter 4 from the Need to capture and create WBS-0. Here is an example:

NEED: Comprehensive automated inventory management structure.

VISION STATEMENT: Deliver a comprehensive inventory structure with a fully operational capability within eighteen months. (Note: This statement is for the software and not a vision associated with the mission and purpose of a company.)

Continuously refer to the CRIT guidelines to uncover the all necessary possible variation and concerns. Using CRIT is a must do process throughout the UDS model.

Establish WBS – 0.
WBS - 0 [Action Verb], [Noun(s)]
    Example: <u>Provide for Inventory Management</u> (Avoid using the system, requirement, capability, etc. because of their ambiguity, but at the same time realize a material solution could surface within the UDS activities.)

Establish WBS – 01
The UDS team determines and establishes WBS-01; refer to CRIT guidelines often during the discussion to ensure asking the right questions.

There are several techniques and modeling activities to achieve the goals. One technique is a round table idea generation activity, where the UDS team members provide their ideas. This process continues to exhaust all ideas. The UDS facilitator guides the discussion to capture ideas and writes them in the form of a list, either handwritten notes or on the whiteboard. No single person in the UDS is to dominate the discussion. Then the team works through the list to generate a Master List WBS-01; these WBS-01 items are now considered Components of the more substantial capability.

Another technique involves having the team interact in the creation of the Master List of potential ideas with the facilitator observing. This technique is valuable in grouping the team for later activities. First, while at their table, desk, etc. the UDS team member writes their idea on a note and then places the notes on the whiteboard. This process continues until no more ideas surface. Then the team interacts in the form of discussion and works through each idea and determines its WBS-01 category. The goal of both techniques is to create the WBS-01.

The UDS team will also create many WBS-02 ideas for use later in the modeling effort. These ideas will eventually go into the Parking Lot. The team deletes some as duplicates.

WBS 0 - Provide for Inventory Management

WBS 01	1.10	Log-In
WBS 01	2.10	Add Products
WBS 01	3.10	Store Products
WBS 01	4.10	Release Products

In Figure 5.0 below note a sample WBS-01 derived from the activities. Yes, it appears as an organizational chart, which is acceptable, but the importance is the identification of the WBS-01 Components. The Figure 5.0 below has 4 WBS 01 listed.

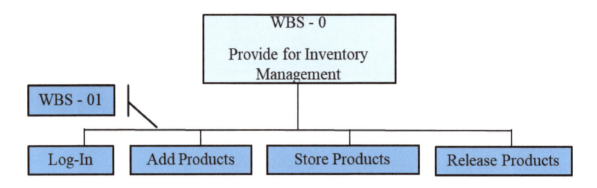

Figure 5.0 WBS-01

At this point in the process the UDS team is to PRIORITIZE the COMPONENTS. Keep in mind the CRIT discussion to get the 1st Component started. The workflow will begin to take shape, but nothing is set in concrete at this juncture. Log-In, in this case, would naturally be the first component for further decomposition for the new capability followed by Add Products, Store Products, and so forth.

Once the UDS team determines the 1st Component for further decomposition the team will capture the component's requirements. This process begins with a master list of user requirements. See Figure 5.1 below for a model of activities necessary for the decomposition of each component. At the end of the first pass through the process for the 1st Component enough information is available to begin the development. Note: All the components are not decomposed at this juncture, only the 1st Component. The goal is to produce a usable product rapidly. Typically, during the process a software developer begins on the

USER-DEFINED SOFTWARE

software as soon as sufficient information is available for coding. The database is also started to communicate data structures and naming conventions for the software developer. Standardization through the enterprise is keen. Standard database naming conventions and file structures eliminates costly data translation in the transportation of information between automated systems.

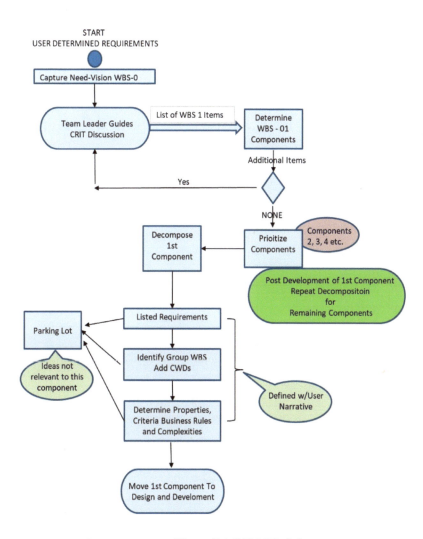

Figure 5.1 WBS Model

USER-DEFINED SOFTWARE

LIST REQUIREMENTS

Once again, the UDS team will use the CRIT method to capture/list the requirements. Use the same technique for establishing the WBS-01 described above. Keep in mind that 2nd; and even 3rd order requirements will surface. Capture them, identify the appropriate component, set aside in the Parking Lot and tag them with the appropriate component. Using the flip charts, whiteboards, etc., capture every idea until the team exhausts the requirements. Just realize the list is dynamic and most likely will change. Once the UDS team captures the list, the next step will be to subdivide into the next level of WBSs as seen below and group them. The facilitator needs to obtain all statements during the discussion. Many of the ideas end up in the Parking Lot for future debate, while some get discarded. Below is an example of a WBS-02/03/04 list for the first component.

WBS 0		Provide for Inventory Management			
WBS 01		Create Log-In			
WBS 02			Establish Log-in Roles		
WBS 02			Ensure Secure Password		
WBS 02			Establish Log-in Time-Out		
WBS 03			Establish Refresh		
WBS 04			Identify User Demographics		
WBS 04			Identify Network Software		

Figure: 5.2 WBS-02/03/04

It is now time to add the CWDs to the list and capture the originator, because during the development it is important to know the originator of the requirement should additional discussion be required. (See Figure 5.3 below) Using the CRIT concept the facilitator needs to interact with the UDS processes to capture CWD for each requirement. During this process each team member offers ideas and considerations. Recall CWD means Critical; Wants and Desires. This is the start of building a Requirement Traceability Matrix (RTM).

	ID #						C/W/D
WBS 0	0.00	Provide for Inventory Management					C
WBS 01	1.10		Create Log-In				C
WBS 02	1.21			Establish Log-in Roles			C
WBS 02	1.22			Ensure Secure Password			C
WBS 02	1.23			Establish Log-in Time-Out			C
WBS 03	1.30			Establish Refresh			W
WBS 04	1.41			Identify User Demographics			W
WBS 04	1.42			Identify Network Software			D

Figure 5.3 CWD Added

The UDS team repeats the process used to decompose the 1st component and each succeeding component to reach the lowest level for the decomposition. In the WBS figure above, the USD team list requirements, then groups them according to where to accomplish them within the overall component. It is important to note once again, the team is NOT to decompose the entire new capability immediately, but instead, when the team has enough data about the 1st component, the development processes, coding the workflow, etc. can occur. The software logic will not be complete until the UDS team define the business rules.

BUSINESS RULES

Within the scope of capturing the requirement don't overlook the need to obtain the business rules. Most often, in the analysis, business rules drive complexity discussed later. Requirements with a significant number of business rules, scientific notation, etc. increase the complexities. Complex metric algorithms increase the complexity.

Before we move into the Design and Development let's finish with Determining the Requirements. Throughout the WBS analysis identify the details for the requirements as properties, criteria and complexity. Once again, use the white board, and a flip chart to work through the identification of the properties and criteria, however, realize the dynamics of process drives change.

DETERMINE the PROPERTIES and CRITERIA and COMPLEXITY

➢ *Properties* is an all-inclusive term to describe and distinguish the complete component. Think of Properties as design characteristic, (e.g., attributes, characteristics, details and features). Assume the capability has a user screen with a requirement for a drop-down box. Use CRIT to elaborate the properties, such as size, location on the screen, and data for the user screen. As the UDS team works through the details, the developers gain a clear picture of what the user wants. The developers with elaborate experience will facilitate establishment of complexity and time intervals as part of the CRIT analysis.

➢ *Criteria* are critical in the decomposition to establish the standards-to-testable metrics along with the roles of the users. The criteria as related to the user screen discussed in properties above depict users' roles and how to access the data. Also, the UDS team gathers testable criteria for measuring product acceptance. One point on testing: If the requirement is not testable, the requirement is too ambiguous and not reliable. Like analyzing the Properties, use CRIT to document complexities.

At this point begin to establish the traceability. It doesn't matter the order for working either the criteria or properties first in the analysis, what matters is to portray the details using any note-taking device. The UDS team can determine the numbering scheme for the requirements to ensure meeting their mission needs. Figure 5.4 below provides a sample to rate the complexities.

> *Complexity* identifies the level of difficulty involved in developing the software for the requirement. The UDS team assigns a complexity rating for each of the requirements. Use a flashcard to score the individual scores and then sum the teams rating into a score for the requirements. Next average the score of the component. Repeat the process for each component. At the end of the complexity analysis, include an average rating for the complexity of the components. Add a product complexity at the end.

In the example, Figure 5.4 below, a scale of 1 being least complex-to- 5 as being the most complex, a diagram could easily be constructed to show the middle average of 2.5. In our example, therefore the overall capability complexity for Inventory Management is 2.41, which is slightly below the middle average and thus a moderately complex score. Determining the complexity scale is at the UDS team discretion, however, use standard variances to determine complexity. For instance, a rating of 0-to-1.9 is simple complex, while 4.1-to-5.0 is very complex and challenging.

Figure 5.4 represents a <u>complete</u> WBS for the project. Notice the complexity of the 1st Component is 2.83. Therefore, it was determined to be the first component for decomposition. As other WBS 02s are decomposed then they are added to the master list of work activities. Retain this master WBS throughout the project and keep it as part of the life cycle documentation.

	ID #						C/W/D	Originator	Complexity
WBS 0	0.00	Provide for Inventory Management					C	Customer	2.41
WBS 01	1.10		Create Log-In				C	UDS Team	2.83
WBS 02	1.21			Establish Log-in Roles			C	User 1	4
WBS 02	1.22			Ensure Secure Password			C	User 2	4
WBS 02	1.23			Establish Log-in Time-Out			C	User 3	3
WBS 03	1.30			Establish Refresh			W	User 4	2
WBS 04	1.41			Identify User Demographics			W	User 5	2
WBS 04	1.42			Identify Network Software			D	User 6	2
WBS 01	2.10		Add Products				C	UDS Team	2.5
WBS 02	2.21			Indentify Product by Bar Code			C	User 1	3
WBS 02	2.22			Add Product Count			C	User 3	3
WBS 03	2.31			Add total value of Products			W	User 6	2
WBS 03	2.32			Calculate Purchase Cost			C	User 4	2
WBS 01	3.10		Store Products						2
WBS 02	3.20			Identify Product Location			C	User 6	2
WBS 03	3.30			Report Inventory Count			C	User 4	2
WBS 01	4.10		Release Products						2.3
WBS 02	4.20			On-Sale Tag for Shipping			C	User 1	3
WBS 03	4.30			Decrease Inventory			C	User 4	2
WBS 04	4.40			Assess Reorder Point			C	User 5	2

Figure 5.4 Complexities

Component > UDS Team ID > Requirement ID > Properties> Criteria > Complexity

(Note: UDS Team ID is necessary in the event more than one team is working on the component.)

USER NARRATIVES

The UDS technical writer documents the business rules, without a large amount of writing during the activities; pictures, drawings are favorable in the process to describe requirements and business rules. (See Use Case Model (UCM) in Annex E.) Throughout the UDS model, the team interacts with the user and their interaction instantiates user interactions. Drawings and pictorials aid in the documentation to include roles of the various users. It is perfectly acceptable to draw each requirement and capture the details. Use role-playing in the process if necessary, to denote the process and workflow, then the team models the workflow to identify the business rules for the requirements. Label each input and output within the model. These labels describe in enough details for coding and database design. The team and technical writer document the properties and criteria in definitions for activities, input and output labels, and business rules along with authority. Towards the end of the project, these documents become part of the life cycle documents.

Defining the testing cases becomes part of the activities. When a WBS is decomposed testable parameters are available. The test professionals use these to build an automated testing process within a chosen automated test tool. Test cases and test databases will enable a thorough and comprehensive test of the total system. These testing activities will not eliminate frequent hands-on testing by the UDS team and other users but facilitate a more thorough test and quality product.

The UDS model favors a strong test process over lengthy requirements and design documentation. The test plan will enable establishing artifacts for life cycle documentation at the end of the project.

Also test professionals are an integral part of the UDS team for delivery of a quality software product. These test professionals are software developers and engineers with a strong background in software development. Testing within the UDS model is the main element to delivery of a quality user acceptable product.

Testing for quality comes with cost, however, it is far less expensive than delivery of a poor product requiring extensive maintenance.

CHAPTER 6 - DEFINING MAINTENANCE DEFECTS

MAINTENANCE DEFECTS

Defining maintenance requirements for software within the UDS model is different from a new capability. Since fielded software is already in production, the user encountered difficulty and submits a defect starting the maintenance activities.

A road map for UDS maintenance activities is in Figure 6.0. Once a user submits the defect, the CRIT process is once again used to analyze the error. Over time, management has assigned the original UDS team to other projects. A few experts most likely remained for continuity. If one or two of the original UDS team members stay for maintenance, this will only strengthen the maintenance UDS team.

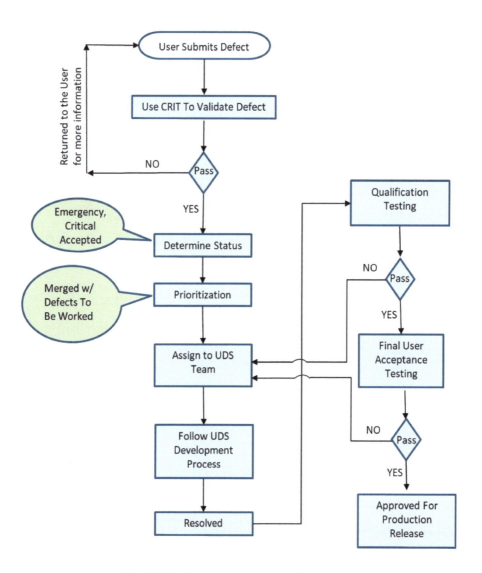

Fig 6.0 Maintenance Process Flow Diagram

USER-DEFINED SOFTWARE

VALIDATION

Using the CRIT process, the UDS team will first validate the defect as being authentic and valid. Should the UDS team be unable to duplicate the fault, then the team will request more detailed information from the User to replicate the error. It is critical to reproduce the error in a laboratory environment to enable the UDS team to make proper repairs. Duplication is essential during software maintenance activities.

DETERMINE STATUS

Next, the UDS team supports the decision regarding the status of the defect. Team lead categorizes defects into basically 3 types:

> *Category I*: Emergency defects receive top priority if loss of life is possible, loss of valuable resources or even sever work stoppage is evident.

> *Category II*: Critical defects are when there is a work around for the problem. These defects require a higher priority than a defect in the accepted category because the work around is cumbersome and is having a major impact on the using community.

> *Category III*: Accepted defects receive the same prioritization process along with other accepted defects.

***Note 1: In the UDS maintenance model where an Emergency CAT I defect is identified, the defect is assigned immediately to a UDS Team for resolution. The goal for the repair and release is 24-hour turn-around time. Team leads must keep a close tab on the software and ensure the fix is accomplished.

***Note 2: Critical defects are those defects that are having a major impact on production. The supporting functional community determines the severity critical defects. Like an emergency defect they may be assigned directly to a UDS team for repair and release.

PRIORITIZATION

These activities occur post defect acceptance. The activities include capturing the existing defects along with other associated work for workload determination activities. If the development team has enough resources, then defect correction activities can occur separately from the new capabilities or enhancements in the development process.

***Note: Ensure any changes made for maintenance are provided to the other teams to avoid costly rework for the same defect.

Three sublevels used in the defect severity prioritization are:

<u>High, Medium and Low</u>.

The following guidelines can be used when assigning severity to software defects within the testing parameters. However, these levels are applicable to errors encountered within the field for defect categorization:

> *"**High** –* System crashes, causes non-recoverable conditions, loss of key component functionality, database or file corruption and potential data loss are all examples of a High severity defect. A new build with fixed high severity defects is required. Testing cannot continue while a High severity defect exists.

> *Medium* – Major system component unusable due to failure or incorrect functionality. Medium severity defects cause serious problems such as a lack of functionality that can have a major impact to the user. Medium severity may prevent other areas or components of the system from being tested. A work round may exist, but the work around is inconvenient or difficult.

> *Low* – Incorrect or incomplete functionality of a component or process. Low business impact if this is not delivered or implemented. These are usually cosmetic issues raised during User Acceptance Testing (UAT)."[17]

CAT I - Emergency High defect is the highest high priority due to its Emergency Condition. Emergencies will **not** have a Medium and Low priority.

While a *CAT II* - Critical-High carries a significant defect rating; releasing the code is important to solve the problem within the user community due

---

[17] T. Cheylene, How to Classify Bug Severity in Your Bug Report, LEAN TESTING, 2005, https://leantesting.com/how-to-classify-bug-severity/

to the troublesome workaround encountered in the field. The UDS team works CAT II Mediums and Lows ahead of CAT III.

For *CAT III* defects a special prioritization process assesses CAT III's to provide their High, Medium and Low priority. The UDS team works on CAT III defects based on prioritization. The functional community prioritizes CAT III's and then groups the defects within their component for repair. For instance, if an Accepted-High is being worked by the coding team, and an Accepted-Low has also been identified in the same section of code, it is encouraged to fix the Accepted-Low defect to save time from a development perspective. This is an important time saving technique to add other defects within the same area for the release. This process is a judgement call and normally the Senior Manager in the using community has an input into the decision.

Prioritization is a controlled process, guided by the using community in the form of a Configuration Board (CB). The CB sets the priority for work. The technical input from the UDS team in terms of cost and schedule are important in the overall decision of workload priority.

ASSIGNED to a UDS TEAM

The assignment process is once again a judgement call by the system Program Manager. If there is more than one UDS team; then use a Team Identification number. The goal is to balance the workload among the teams.

However, for some development activities, the development team consist of one or two developers. In this case, the work assignment is purely sequential in the order determined by the CB. On the other hand, if there exist more than one team then the assignment has several considerations. The key to determining the team is based on keeping key metrics for the team and to determine the **Delivery Interval** for the delivery of the capability discussed in Chapter 9 - Metrics.

Just as seen at the end of the process for determining the requirements for a New Capability, once a maintenance item is identified the work to repair the defect must begin.

SPECIAL note for maintenance and a major enhancement. Any and all repairs accomplished in maintenance must be rendered in the enhancement. This is important to maintain complete functionality in the enhancement. At some point in the development of the new enhancement a decision is required to put a hold on adding new maintenance repairs due to the release of the enhancement. It is a judgement call but important in the release of the enhancement.

CHAPTER 7 - DESIGN, DEVELOPMENT, AND USER TESTING (DDUT)

ITERATIONS VERSUS INCREMENT

A lot of work has been done thus far in the generation of the components and requirements. But Design, Development, and User Testing (DDUT) in the UDS Model is the bridge from the requirements generation activities in the WBS discussion to the actual product.

Understanding two key essential terms and the difference between Iteration and

USER-DEFINED SOFTWARE

Increment are critical for working with the UDS model:

> *ITERATION*: An iteration stems from a repeatable process (DDUT activities) to produce a single requirement.

> *INCREMENT*: An increment is the consolidation of iterations or a single iteration, such as for an Emergency Defect into a releasable/deliverable product to the users.

DDUT activities are in one iteration. The entire component is not coded at once, but parts of the component are coded in a two-week work package. This enables small portions of the requirement to be built and tested. Eventually the entire component will be completed through iteration development. Note: a two-week work package is the minimum duration of an iteration and preferred. Four weeks is the maximum. Staggering work package durations are acceptable if the results do not delay other development activities.

The UDS Model built around cohesion and collaboration throughout the events sets the foundations for success. However, in DDUT activities, collaboration can't be over emphasized. DDUT is not separated into defined blocks of activities as in the Waterfall Model, but all-inclusive with the UDS team held intact. Design and development start almost simultaneously. Testing is continuous; however, User Testing (either manual or automated) is a separate function. Concurrence by the user signals completion for the iteration.

One point to put into perspective is the architectural design of software. Architecture in software is different than architecture in the design of automobiles, buildings, bridges, aerospace vehicles, ships etc. Architecture in these disciplines enable the creation of a scaled model. The model enables presentation in a visual display, even a handheld model, before full scale production. Creating a scaled model is not the case in the design of software.

A prototype model in software would be as a measure to test the development and gain assurance of the process. The programmer or developer writes the software code (program) in a visual form such as the pages of a book. The software language is known to the software developer through years of experience. The written code, produced by either a software developer or artificial intelligence, and viewable by the human eye, is called source code. Once the developed software (written code) is compiled using a software language compiler, it then becomes object code in digital, electronic, executable, and binary form.

The execution of the software on the other hand results in a Graphical User Interface (GUI), or a printed output product for the user. The UDS team develops the software based on user needs and requirements generated during the activities to obtain the details for each requirement discussed in previous chapters.

DESIGN

Fundamentally design is a crucial portion of the development from a user perspective. Design focus on the GUI used or interacted with the user. Like generating requirements, the design is heavily dependent on the Users (Front-Line, Functional, and Corporate) working side-by-side with the development team to ensure the exactness and flow of the GUI. One note from capturing the requirement, is the screen designs (GUIs) will not have functioning coded logic. They are simple screens, even hand drawings will work to articulate the flow and capture the information.

Software development includes the code and database structures along with other artifacts. Both the database and software code must be uniform and consistent; else the user will not have a successful experience. The UDS team uses the UDS processes to deliver every element contained within the GUI/Printed Product/Query etc.

DEVELOPMENT

A key element for the UDS process is team availability, during the entire development process working towards the goal. The minimum collaboration team meeting is twice a week, where the team has the chance to review the work accomplished from a coding perspective and review pending actions. Tuesday and Thursday have worked well for these collaborative meetings.

Even though in Incremental Development (Figure 7.0), Design, Development, and User Testing appears as blocks, these activities are continuous with constant feedback. The UDS team builds Use Case Models as described later in Annex E. The UDS team must capture the Properties and Criteria (specific details) during the modeling, to ensure software development for each property and criterion. While capturing the properties and criteria is painstaking, incorporating them into the product is essential for the successful development of the iteration and increment, leading to the delivery of the product/capability into a system.

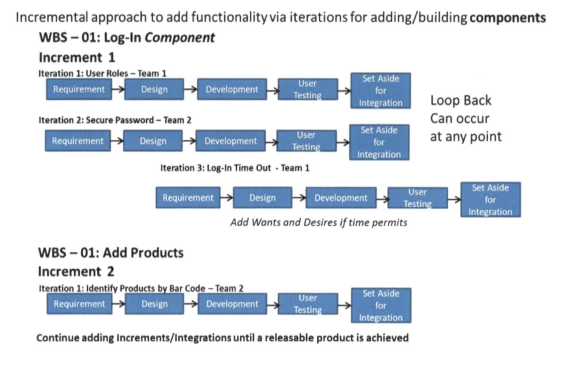

Figure 7.0 Incremental Development Model

Requirements>Properties> Criteria > Complexity>Iteration
Iterations>Increments> Components >Products>Capabilities>Systems

Continue adding WBS-01 components until the product is ready for a release.

Once the product is ready or any portion of the product is ready for release then promote the software to Integration.

(Note: The above box headings are excellent labels for Kanban to track the work or any tool of choice.)

TESTING

The key to success in the UDS model is testing, especially a joint test between the developer and the users. Traditional software development has a test function called Unit Testing conducted by the developer. This type of testing is still a critical part of UDS model and is a part of the development process. Within the UDS model; *Iteration Testing*, the user is highly active in the process and testing is continuous. The user tests the product in User Testing. Without user satisfaction of the product iteration work continues.

Every requirement in each iteration requires concurrence by the user in the User Testing activity. Until the user concurs, the product continues to be recycled in the form of a loopback until the user is satisfied with the product. User satisfaction signals the concurrence by the user for the iteration.

Once an iteration passes user testing, then it is set aside for either adding additional iterations or is grouped with other iterations for further testing.

In *Incremental Testing*, the team test all planned increment for the release. Every increment must receive user concurrence before the product moves into Integration Testing.

Integration Testing is included as part of the DDUT because the UDS team is still highly involved in the process at this point. It takes careful *Configuration Management (CM)* to ensure the product merges the All Increments.

Note: In cases where only one increment is targeted for the release, then the merger in the integration process contains one iteration. The increment may include a single product as in the case of an Emergency Defect.

USER-DEFINED SOFTWARE

Figure 7.1 Integration Activities

➤ **Integration testing:** This testing comes to play in the Integration activities once the Merger is complete for all the Increments 1, 2, 3 etc.

➤ **Integrated Incremental Testing:** Once the product is assembled by CM the UDS team, primarily the developers, will test the product to provide assurance the proper elements, coded version etc. are in the release product.

➤ **User Testing:** The UDS user team members are responsible for the User testing at this point in the UDS model for the increment(s) in the release. This testing includes both functional testing and qualification testing. Any difficulties encountered are sent back in the form of a Recycle for further coding etc. until the UDS team corrects the error.
(Note: It is important to not consider User Testing conducted in Integration portion of the UDS model as the Final Acceptance Testing, since the testing is done by the UDS team.)

➤ **Automated testing** can serve the needs for a larger release, but it requires **DEDICATED** developers to maintain the automated tool and the test environments. Automated testing is valuable for small maintenance release to test other portions of the system to ensure the maintenance software didn't affect other components; referred to as regression testing. A front-end user might be able to keep the tool up to date, but the best solution is to have technical test tool experts as part of the UDS team. Their longevity is just as valuable as other team members. (See Test Planning in Annex A)

Once User Testing is complete in Integration, the CM assembles the product to promote the product to the Acceptance Environment for Final Acceptance Testing conducted in the Implementation portion of the UDS model.

To see the Test Environments and various roles refer the Annex B – Testing Steps, along with Annex C - Types of Environments.

UDS DDUT for MAINTENANCE

The UDS team follows the UDS process for development regardless of the type of development: New Capability or Maintenance. The key is to realize that the effort is to begin once a clear understanding of the maintenance need is fully understood. The difference is to use the Defect (ID/Name) in the iteration identification. The Increment ID can take on a numeric value for tracking purpose. The UDS DDUT process is the same for maintenance, to include delivery.

SECURITY

Good software goes beyond DDUT to meet users' needs and requirements. An important criterion is the security aspects.

USER-DEFINED SOFTWARE

When building a new capability, UDS recommends using Security and Privacy Controls for Federal Information Systems and Organizations, NIST Special Publication 800-53, Revision 4.[18] It is best to <u>build security upfront</u> in the development of new capability than to wait until the end. UDS recommends NIST controls become high-level requirements in the development process to ensure the highest level of security. For other considerations in security refer the National Institute of Standards and Technology (NIST)[19] and search for Cyber Security and Information Technology.

Security in the UDS model is also based on accomplishing vulnerability scans to identify coding weakness and security measures. The software must be secure or else expect a miserable experience. Scanning the software before the release is essential. The scans will identify specific logic vulnerabilities require correcting ahead of the software release. The network likewise needs to have an accurate scan for network vulnerabilities.

Within software maintenance, the UDS team must add security control as an iteration to complete the security needs.

RISK

---

[18] Use Security and Privacy Controls for Federal Information Systems and Organizations, NIST Special Publication 800-53, Revision 4., Joint Task Force Transformation Initiative https://nvlpubs.nist.gov/nistpubs/SpecialPublications/NIST.SP.800-53r4.pdf

[19] National Institute of Standards and Technology (NIST), https://www.nist.gov

USER-DEFINED SOFTWARE

Managing Risk is never easy but the best way to reduce the risk is to work it as a collaborative team to consider all the positive and negative aspects. The CRIT questions are important and must be accomplished as related to risk. Risk is inherent in any project but risk is manageable as long as the potential or probability is identified. Risk management tools help identify the risk for a project along with mitigations.

Critical areas for risk consideration are: Interfaces, Governing Climate, Resources and Security:

- ➢ Interfaces always seems to be the least of concern in systems, but if not understood will produce a poorly accepted product.

- ➢ Policy is a risk due to the frequency of changing leadership, but also from excessive leadership involvement and control of the work.

- ➢ Resource management is a dynamic risk due to the nature of change in technology and loss of assets.

- ➢ Security in the realm of technology must remain high on the radar as technology continues to expand and change.

CHAPTER 8 - IMPLEMENTATION

Implementation is the final stage of the UDS model. From a software perspective the Figure 8.1 below is a simple guide to move the software through the UDS model for implementation.

Figure 8.1 Implementation

Like in the Integration activities described in DDUT, the CM is responsible for the configuration of the product for the final push to Acceptance Environment. (See

USER-DEFINED SOFTWARE

Annex C - Types of Environments for the different environments from Development into Production Environment.

Once again, a quick check by the UDS team is necessary and then Quality Testing is conducted by an independent team. This is important from the UDS model to ensure the product is meeting expectations. Once the Quality Team concurs then the product is moved for Final Acceptance Testing. Also, throughout the UDS model testing is highly dependent on users testing the software. In the final acceptance of the software, a different <u>set of users</u> (*stakeholders*) are charged with the Final Acceptance Testing of the software.

An automated test tool will enable a through test; however, the output must be consistent and meet expectations. If the upgrade is for an enhancement and historical test transactions are available, then run the test transactions into both the older software and the newer version. Compare the outputs of both tests. The results must match or the UDS team must be able to explain the difference. If the UDS cannot explain the difference, then further problem analysis is needed to determine the reason or reasons for the difference. <u>Release of new software where these tests results do not match is not recommended</u>.

Final acceptance testing is a total test to make sure associated documentation and other necessary artifacts needed for the implementation are thoroughly checked for accuracy.

System Testing is necessary for an end-to-end system check. This test is often overlooked but in a major modification it is critical to make sure the total system works and performs as required along with interfaces. One other item in the system test is to determine if the software is performing properly through a performance evaluation.

Finally deliver the product into production.

Implementation is a major undertaking that must begin at the start at the UDS model. It is important to begin the identification of implementation activities and artifacts needed to ensure a smooth implementation. Other considerations for the Implementation should include:

> Contingencies for a fall back capability, in the event a process is missed,

> Security issues, these requirements are part of the development actions,

> Interface checks are always part of Implementation especially in final acceptance testing,

> Documentation such as a User Manual for a new capability or an updated User Manual for maintenance defect,

> Test Plan and test scripts.

Keep in mind Implementation is just as critical for the success of the software delivery as the actual creation of the software. Use the same type of analysis for Needs and Requirements to list items for consideration in implementing the software.

A failed implementation is as much a failure of the project as errors in the software. Plan early for the implementation to ensure successful implementation.

USER-DEFINED SOFTWARE

What is the definition of DONE? 'Done' simply stated is when the acceptance criteria are complete and ready to proceeding into acceptance testing. UDS on the other hand firmly believes the definition of 'Done' is when the user accepts and implements the software product without errors.

CHAPTER 9 - METRICS

CRIT ESTIMATION – COST and DELIVERY TIME INTERVAL

The delivery interval for a UDS team determines the speed for the delivery of the capability. The timeline is not intended to chastise team members but used for assignment of new work in the delivery of the capability. Three factors play an important role in the delivery interval:

First is the complexity. Refer to the requirement process to assess the original complexity. The degree of the complexity of the component has a large impact on the resolution of any defect. The most important aspect of fixing a defect in a highly complex component is the test time. Testing is critical because the entire component requires aggressive testing.

➢ Second is the skill level. Skills are always important when it comes to software development both technical development and functional skills. The UDS team needs to maintain a high level of skills simply because without the proper skill sets the risk is increased.

➢ Third is a clear understanding of the iteration or defect and the coding necessary to complete the task. This is closely coupled with the proper skills but the understanding of the required coding for a new capability or maintenance needs is extremely important in calculating the delivery time interval.

➢ Fourth is the need for collaboration during the coding activities. Recall the UDS model is built around frequent collaboration.

Below is a simple technique to calculate the Delivery Time (DT) interval. Use this technique for the estimation and prediction. It doesn't matter if one or multiple teams are on the project the technique works equally the same. These are the formulas for the UDS metrics:

Actual Time minus Estimated Time = Delivery Time:
AT/ET = DT Percentage

To determine the **BUDGET ADJUSTMENT,** use the percentages in this manner.

Budget ($$$) x DT Percentage = Adjustments (Either in a saving or additional need).

Let's work through an example to see the results.

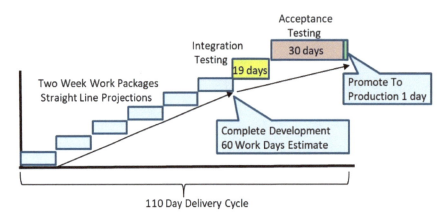

Figure 9.0 Delivery Time

DELIVERY TIME INTERVAL ESTIMATION VERSUS ACTUALS

A one work week equals 5 days.

In this example, delivery of product on-time at 110 days, produces a DT % of 1 which is a perfect score and a Delivery Time (DT) interval of 0, which means no deviations from the planned delivery.

Assume the product is delivered under **schedule** at 104 days means a value of .89 or 12% faster.

(104Actual/110 Estimate = .945 DT value or 5.4545 % faster)

Assume the product is **delivered late** in 122 days, means a value of 1.11

(rounded) or 11% behind schedule.

(122 Actual/110 Estimate = 1.109 DT value or 11% behind schedule [rounded up])

The above is considered a straight-line estimate as compared to the one that varies. However, the actual timeline may vary and thus there is a need to show the actual line. In the next example, notice the adjustment is based on a delay in the delivery of a work package. Even if other teams are meeting expectations, the delay of one work package affects the total delivery timeline. Thus, an actual timeline is needed, and the projection is adjusted.

The diagram below shows how the delay of a work package affects the delivery.

Notice the 4th work package is shown as having a 10 day (2-weeks of additional work = late delivery.) This delay is then used to estimate the future actual delivery. Also, the integration time was delayed by two days.

At the time the 4th Work Package was delivered, the estimation for the extra 2 day for integration was not known. Therefore, logically, the second delivery time interval was off by 2 days. The purpose of the graph is intended to show the total time the project took was 122 days.

USER-DEFINED SOFTWARE

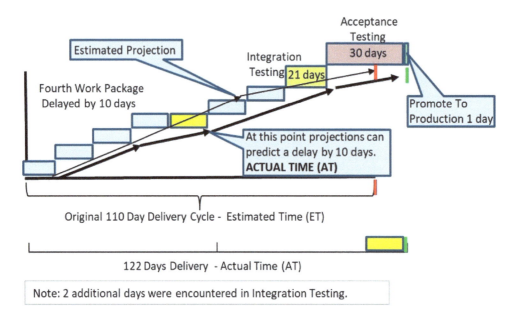

Figure 9.1 Delayed Delivery

To determine the **BUDGET ADJUSTMENT,** use the actuals in this manner.

Our project has an estimate of $150,000 over a period of 110 days which means the daily cost for the project is ($150,000/110 = $1,363.64 per day (rounded))

Assume the budget for the project was $150,000.

Faster delivery produced a saving of **$8,181.82:**

> **(104 Actual days x $1,363.64 = $141,818.18 Actual Cost).**

Estimated Cost minus Actual Cost yields a saving of $8,181.82

Another means is to multiply the daily cost by the number of days saved

(6 days x $1,363.64 yields $8,181.84) The 2 cents difference is due to the daily computation from rounding.

Using the percentage can produce an equivalent amount but there will be a minor rounding issue. ($150,000 x .054545 = $$8,181.75).

USER-DEFINED SOFTWARE

For accuracy recommend using the actual values in lieu of percentages.

Late delivery produces a budget need of **$16,350**

($150,000 x 1.109 = $166,350 - $150,000 = $16,350 based on percentages.

Actuals on the other hand produce a budget need of $16,363.68 (12 days late times $1,363.64 yields the value of $16,363.68 over cost.)

<u>Recommend using the actuals for the cost analysis for more precise accuracies.</u>

Our cost expectations at the end of 8 weeks (40 days x 1,363.64) = $54,545.60

However, the actual number of days is 10 weeks or 50 days (50 days x 1,363.64 = $68.182.00) at the first identification of a delay. It is easy to see that a cost overrun is occurring after 10 weeks of work.

It is best to use the actual figures to the analysis due to the rounding errors associated with percentages.   Percentages are okay for Senior level briefing but not for actual cost.

This method is much simpler to use than other estimating techniques to include calculating planned estimates versus actuals variances in terms of percentages.

Because there was a delay, it is also important to assess the reason for the delay. The factors mentioned above are acceptable for conducting an evaluation. The goal is to gain an understanding of causes and make appropriate adjustments in future estimations. The cause might be as simple as underestimating the complexity of the requirement for this work package.

Several analysis techniques are available to conduct the evaluation for why the delivery was late. Below is a Problem Resolution Diagram for problem resolution based on CRIT. There are numerous other tools for problem resolutions. Regardless of the tool chosen, the goal is to find a recommendation for a solution.

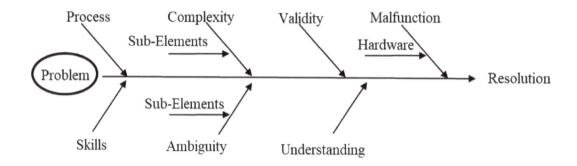

Figure 9.2 CRIT Problem Analysis Diagram

PRODUCTIVE MANAGEMENT (PdM) VS. PROCESS MANAGEMENT (PcM)

UDS favors measurement of productivity over process management. Productivity metrics enable the identification of when a team is at its maximum performance. Identifying and measuring productivity is the goal. Also, a team leader, through assessing productivity, can identify process improvements to eliminate wasted activities. From a metric perspective the Law of Diminishing Returns[20] comes into play in the assessment. Understanding this principle enables management to determine a level of productivity performance.

The Figure 9.0 above show a high level of productivity during the development of

---

[20] My Accounting Course, https://www.myaccountingcourse.com/accounting-dictionary/law-of-diminishing-returns

the product. PdM is a measurement of production. Notice the similarity of the production graphs in this chapter to the graph below representing a metric graph for the Law of Diminishing Return.[21]

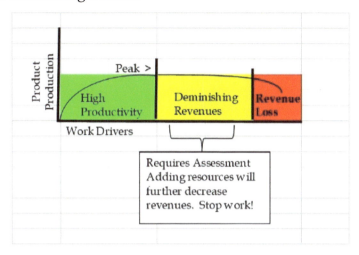

Figure 9.3 Productivity Measure

When any any form of work peaks in terms of performance, adding more work, people etc., will yield negative results and returns on the investment. Careful assessment of productivity is needed to maximize both productivity and cost. Adding more human resources is not necessarily the answer. At some point the cost of production, by adding resources, eventually produces a loss in revenue as the total output reduces.[22]

KEY UDS METRICS

➤ Acceptance Testing Errors,

➤ Cost to Deliver,

---

[21] Celestine Chau, "Law of Diminishing Returns", Personal Excellence, https://personalexcellence.co/blog/law-of-diminishing-returns/
[22] My Accounting Course, https://www.myaccountingcourse.com/accounting-dictionary/law-of-diminishing-returns

- ➤ Defects by Category,

- ➤ Delivery Time,

- ➤ Errors in Testing,

- ➤ Help Desk Calls,

- ➤ Help Desk Resolution,

- ➤ Integration Testing Errors,

- ➤ Number of Components per Iteration,

- ➤ Number of Defects,

- ➤ Number of loop backs,

- ➤ Number of Iterations,

- ➤ Number of Increments,

- ➤ Performance Measurement,

- ➤ Quality Factors,

- ➤ System Analysis from Errors.

The key and important aspects for metrics are the identification of improvement opportunities. For instance, if a series of help desk calls points to one screen, then an assessment of the screen is necessary to determine the reason for the numerous help desk calls.

USER SURVEY

Complete a user survey at the end of each release. The main items for the survey will focus on user satisfaction of the product. The product in the hands of the user will pinpoint user's satisfaction. Ask pointed leading questions:

- ➤ Did problems gets resolved timely,

- ➤ Did the product meet expectations,

USER-DEFINED SOFTWARE

➢ Did the user documentation meet expectations,

➢ Length of time using the software,

➢ Was the product easy to use and follow,

➢ Was the product on time,

➢ Was the team friendly and helpful,

➢ Were the implementation instructions complete,

➢ What was the quality of the product?

Have generic rating scale from Poor (1) to Excellent (5).

Avoid any and all gender related questions.

CHAPTER 10 - UDS DOCUMENTATION

The UDS framework and methodology would be incomplete without addressing the need for documentation. UDS like Agile framework favor a correct product that meets the user's needs and requirements. Within software engineering documentation is the overarching terms used for all the documentation.

There are numerous books written about documentation. The following link provides a good list of documentation and provides a template for each.
http://sce2.umkc.edu/BIT/burrise/pl/appendix/Software_Documentation_Templates/

USER-DEFINED SOFTWARE

Within the UDS framework, it is essential to document during the process rather than an elaborate upfront documentation process. The link below has an excellent chart for reference. While it has a Copyright listed on the graph, it is still a unique diagram to show the documentation between traditional processes versus the present-day models and the UDS framework.

http://www.agilemodeling.com/essays/agileDocumentationBestPractices.htm

The UDS promotes the documentation of needs, and then work through the requirement into a WBS. Also, the UDS framework institutionalizes the need for a Program or Project Management Directive (PMD). The PMD is crucial to ensure the establishment of the team through appointments and identification of roles.

UDS framework and methodologies for each iteration institutes early documentation of the design, and development of the code, along with the creation of both Use Case Model (UCM) (See Annex E-Use Case Model).

The technical writer is an essential member of the UDS team. Notice the Technical Writer is an actor in the sample USE CASE in Annex E. The Technical Writer has the role in consolidating the documents at the end of each iteration. It may be wise to have more than one technical writer on the team.

UDS recommend a small set of documents for the life cycle process to ensure the product history is maintained.

USER-DEFINED SOFTWARE

Documentation includes these artifacts:

- ➤ Component History (backlog)
- ➤ Defect History and Changes
- ➤ Design Specifications for Iterations
- ➤ Productivity Metrics
- ➤ Program Management Directive
- ➤ Release Authority
- ➤ Requirements Traceability
- ➤ Security Assessment
- ➤ Source Code Library
- ➤ Team Composition
- ➤ Test Documentation
- ➤ User Acceptance
- ➤ User Surveys

CHAPTER 11 - PRODUCT LINES

WHAT IS A PRODUCT OR A PRODUCT LINE?

It is challenging to communicate capability without a discussion on a Product.

A product by definition is the results of a series of activities to produce either a tangible or non-tangible product.

"1. A good, idea, method, information, object or service created as a result of a process and serves a need or satisfies a want. It has a combination of tangible and intangible attributes (benefits, features, functions, uses) that a seller offers a buyer for purchase. For example, a seller of a toothbrush not only offers the physical product but also the idea that the consumer will be improving the health of their teeth.

2. Law: A commercially distributed good that is (1) tangible personal property, (2) output or result of a fabrication, manufacturing, or production process, and (3) passes through a distribution channel before being consumed or used.

3. Marketing: A good or service that most closely meets the requirements of a particular market and yields enough profit to justify its continued existence."[23]

The product line coupled with the vision and objects set the path for manufacturing and development of a product. Using the Saturn Rocket Program think of the massive industrialization and diverse product lines needed for the overall project. Each primary subsystem, rocket engines, fuel tanks, capsule, space suits, landing craft, etc. were all unique product lines. The overarching product (Saturn Rocket) required assembly of the unique products in the subsystems like stacking building blocks.

This massive project had a stringent specification in the manufacturing of the subsystems; else the assemble would fail. Not only were the standards for the assembly required, but their uniformity for space was likewise part of the manufacturing. These subsystems built their capability and delivered them for testing and assemble. An important point distinguishes the building of these subsystems from a production line process. While a limited number of Saturn Rockets were produced, the product line processes used for the creation of millions of consumer products is not different.

---

[23] Business Dictionary, Product, http://www.businessdictionary.com/definition/product.html

USER-DEFINED SOFTWARE

Consumer products also follow stringent manufacturing specifications; however, the creation of a marketable product line goes through a different series of activities before the product reaches mass production. Like in the creation of a new software product, a need generation process occurs. A new product team of experts will assess the needs and determine the resourcefulness (e.g., production cost versus marketing for profit the product) for the new product line or even a change to an existing product. (Note: The product team of experts will include corporate consumers due to the need for potential patent protections etc. These consumers are considered the users of the product.)

Eventually, the product has a prototype built. Then it undergoes an assessment by the product team. The product team checks it for safety as one of the many aspects for selling of a consumer product. Also, wear and tear type testing, crash testing within the automobile industry are a few of the product testing activities accomplished. The product team will offer and make appropriate alteration before the new product is introduced in a test within a sample market survey. This sampling method is designed to achieve and obtain user assessment and satisfaction feedback. The product team explores all aspects of preparing a consumer product from eye-catching cosmetic appeal-to-affordability by the target user. The product line goes through these huge steps and processes before it ever reaches the shelf of the marketplace. The resulting products all went through a similar process to achieve the creation of a marketable product. But where do new products originate?

Origination of new products is the innovating aspects of a consumer for more modern and better products. Many new products come from new ideas and changes to improve existing products. Market assessments provide improvement opportunities, identifies waste of raw material not needed or used as part of the product. An example, the cardboard part of the candy bar wrapping gave way to a different type of wrapping. In some cases, another non-sticking agent replaced the cardboard wrapping because the cardboard eventually became discarded. Another aspect of market assessment identifies overproduction of products never consumed by the user and eventually exceeded its shelf life.

Mass production of products come from product line assemblies and creating a repeatable process. The repeatable reproduction has been the heart of standardization from the first rifle-to- present-day automobile manufacturing. Production line process for a product is different than the creation of unique subsystems, as was the case with the Saturn Rocket Project. However, like the Saturn Rocket project, production line processes demand standardization. Manufacturing of bottles, cans, paper, etc. all followed a standard process. The lost art of industrial engineering was keen in the establishment of the standard efficient production lines.

How does the product and production line assemble relate to the realm of information technology? Technology product lines range from hardware, software, types of data, and networks are the essential elements of information technology. Innovations in artificial intelligence, augmented reality, robotics, etc. are emerging, and all have defined product lines.

Recently the focus shifted to the product from the consumers perspective and less on the assembling of the product in the production line. Like the manufacturing of a marketable product briefly discussed above, both the product and production for information technology are important to bring new and innovative products to the consumer or to enhance an existing product. How to rekindle the speed and quality for software delivery require a dynamic change in the overall physical layout of the establishment producing the product. This change is encapsulated below as a continuance of the UDS model.

SOFTWARE POCKET FACTORY

Referring to the Saturn Rocket project for the development of the software systems such as the Abort Guidance System (AGS), CORONA or LUMINARY[24] for example, were not developed in a single software factory or one large software factory. These software packages were all product lines for the Saturn Rocket Program and accomplished in a contained unique software pocket factory, to produce the product. These pocket factories were all uniform in their development and delivery. While a pocket factory for software is a unique environment, it is a factory just as much as the sublevel factory in the physical construction of the subsystems in the Saturn Rocket Program. (Note: The use of the term 'pocket' is a new term within the domain of software and a factory, it stems from gem mining in the Rocky Mountains. The miners look for crevasses (pockets) in the side of the mountains to find gems.)

The pocket software factory must have a **VISION STATEMENT**: A short one-liner and include three essential parts:

Part 1: Unify:
The Vision Statement must consist of unifying all-inclusive terms. The

---

[24] David Hoag, "The History of Apollo On-board Guidance, Navigation, and Control", September 1976.

team performing the work must be included. If the team is left out of the vision statement, then it is blasé, non-binding and non-committal.

Part 2: Communicate:

The Vision Statement must communicate an actionable performance or work performed by the community or organization.

Part 3: Integrate:

The vision statement must integrate the resulting processes within the community providing the work with expectations of purpose.

Closely related to the vision statement are the **objectives**, which provide measurable results.

The expected successes are performance criteria to achieve the objectives as it relates to the vision statement. Superlatives such as increase or grow are difficult to measure with a degree of expected success. These types of words cannot be linked to a <u>measurable objective</u> to achieve the vision.

- Objectives communicate a variety of measurable results.
- Objectives are clear and definable; they are measurable.
- Objectives typically are associated with dollars, time, and quality.
- Objectives often relate to measuring accomplishments in terms of percentages of gains from delivery of a product.

SOFTWARE POCKET FACTORY PRODUCT LINE

USER-DEFINED SOFTWARE

The software pocket factory may contain more than one product line. Envision a city block with several extensive facilities and secured drive-in entrances. In an industry, such an establishment would be labeled a plant with a plant manager. Similarly, this city block could be called a software plant and like industry with the same leadership structures. Each facility within the software plant would be labeled a software pocket factory. Then within each of the pocket factory, there could be more than one product lines in the development and delivery of software. Each software product factory needs a simple vision statement, and each product line likewise needs a vision statement. Objectives and metrics are uniform through all product factories and product lines.

Historically, the software was developed and delivered by independent groups. Each group brought a specialized service such as the development, testing, and even independent testing, and last a group would packaging the product for delivery. For efficiencies in the pocket factory, some activities must be self-contained within the pocket factory. For instance, why should a product be moved to a release point outside the pocket factory, then redistributed to the user? Redistribution through the mail service works well in the retail market, but it is not efficient in the delivery of software. The pocket factory needs the skill within its boundary to accomplish the delivery task once the product owner clears the software for release. Accomplishing all <u>tasks</u> within the pocket factory is efficient. Using outside capabilities such as assembling a product and pushing a button for delivery is a waste of resources. Continual delivery of a product comes closer to reality by eliminating wasteful steps for delivery.

Efficiencies and product assurance are likewise needed within the pocket factory to promote user's satisfaction. Every product requires thorough testing, which is a process within itself. However, test developers and software engineers within the software development pocket factory perform the code for automated testing. While this is a time-consuming step, the continual delivery of products must ensure the quality of the product and system continued performance. <u>Testing can't be overstated</u>.

All products are built around a particular set of standards for delivery and have specific deliverable and survival criteria for each of the software products. The development of the software within pocket factories and product lines must be uniform to eliminate the creation of stovepipe systems and capabilities. The uniformity often referred to as standards are the building blocks of uniformity. The value of consistency is for cross-exchange of information but not the resources. It is a waste of resources to expect technical skills to move from one pocket factory to another and be efficient immediately. This is not to say technical resources can't move to another factory or even product line, but if a move does occur, don't set immediate expectations. Software developers, database experts, test developers, etc. gain system related knowledge over time, and their experience is valuable.

Pocket factory product lines are technology-driven, and it is through technology that enables user needs and business rules to improve efficiencies and performance.

USER-DEFINED SOFTWARE

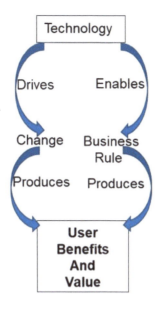

Figure 11.0 Technology

Remember this golden rule in implementing technology for software development and delivery of capability:

DON'T BREAK THINGS.

INNOVATION

Pocket factory product line will continually seek improvements in both processes and toolset to produce software. Stagnation will lead to the loss of the development edge and advantage. Future software development inevitably will bring new toolsets for development of software. Artificial intelligence (AI) with voice command-line instructions eliminating the keystroke process is rapidly approaching reality. Tools that can interpret a screen and produce the code will revolutionize the development. Scanning code into an AI database as a code repository beyond the source code repository will enable swift changes, enhance testing followed by faster delivery.

FRIENDLY HACKING

Finally, hacking is a new domain of testing for software where typical hackers will attempt to invade the system. Friendly hacking is designed to enable exclusive trusted skill sets to try to hack into the software with known hacking techniques. The idea for friendly hacking is to seek security answers, because if our friendly hackers can invade the software, then other hackers can also break into the software.

SWIM LANES

It is important in the pipeline of delivery to always make a conscience decision to keep major activities in separate distinct swim lanes. When working with information technology or any other project separate major activities:

BUYING from BUILDING from OPERATING from MAINTAINING from SUSTAINING.

These actions are separate from each other with different roles and purpose. Their vision statement will likewise be different and so will their focus. In a large organization, such a Department of Defense for example, to have these activities contained under one organizational umbrella creates a rice bowls and affects mission readiness. If the decision is made to buy a technology then let the acquisition begin, but if the decision is to build a capability then let the development begin. Similarly, once the delivery of the capability is accomplished then the Operational stakeholders takes ownership of the delivered product. Just like buying a new car. Once the car buyer takes ownership, they need to have regular maintenance such as changing the oil. It is important to separate maintenance from sustainment because sustainment in the automobile industry would be items of repair identified through the dealership's recall program.

These distinctions are the same within information technology. Keeping them separate is needed for efficiencies.

CONCLUSION

The information contained within these short pages is intended to provide a guide for software development. The intent is to provide the lost skill of the modeling software and then use those models for a quality software system meeting the needs of the user.

Lastly, new ideas for the future of information technology products in a Pocket Factory is essential to the rapid delivery of quality, cost-effective software with speed and efficiencies. Also, process consolidations in the form of uniform teams to complete the delivery is not a new idea but will ultimately reduce delivery times. Within the walls of the pocket factory are two new disciplines with one for an automated test developer, and the other one for friendly hackers. Finally, on the horizon for software development will be artificial intelligence to produce the code.

USER-DEFINED SOFTWARE

Perhaps one of the most significant visions statement was the one from President Kennedy, "First, I believe that this nation should commit itself to achieving the goal, before this decade is out, of landing a man on the moon and returning him safely to the earth."[25]

Vision is asking for a commitment of the nation, to land a man on the moon and return him safely [performance objective]; by the end of the decade [time objective].

The vision for UDS is the future delivery of quality software to meet the immediate needs of the users.

The UDS Model in Annex E introduces a new concept for modeling a work center or a production line. The model points to productivity in the delivery of products.

The UDS development framework and methodology in Annex D is simple model to deliver a quality product. It is in concert with DevSecOps.

UDS favor:

Drivers over Inputs;

Work over Activities;

Products over Outputs

UDS VISION: DELIVER USER-ORIENTED PRODUCTS

---

[25] John F. Kennedy Presidential Library and Museum, Historical Speeches, Address to Joint Session of Congress, May 25, 1961, https://www.jfklibrary.org/learn/about-jfk/historic-speeches/address-to-joint-session-of-congress-may-25-1961

ANNEX A – DOCUMENTATION EXAMPLES

The UDS framework and methodology would be incomplete without addressing the need for documentation. UDS, like Agile, framework favors a correct product that meets user's needs and requirements. Within software engineering documentation are overarching terms used for all the documentation.

Below are UDS examples of key documents.

CONFIGURATION MANAGEMENT

CMP EXAMPLE

CONFIGURATION MANAGEMENT PLAN (CMP)

For

Template Example

dd/mm/yyyy

Name _____
Project Configuration Manager

Name_____
Program Manager

Name_____
Lead Engineer

Name_____
Customer (Acknowledgement)

TABLE OF CONTENTS

Build the table of content to the UDS team's own unique specifications.

Introduction

The Configuration Management Plan (CMP) is very critical to the UDS model and perhaps one of the most important documents for the UDS team.

USER-DEFINED SOFTWARE

Purpose and Scope

Describe the purpose of the CMP and add the scope in terms of the system or systems to be supported by the CMP.

Key Terminology

Add definitions as applicable to the operations and systems. The definitions are to enhance the understanding of the UDS model and the CMP in general.

Organization

Within this portion of the CMP briefly describe the organization and the flow of the software. A graph is very useful for clearly portraying the organizations required for the successful UDS model.

Responsibility and Authority

Items in this section need to include who has the responsibilities for various portions of the UDS model. Also be very specific in terms of expectations and duties. Items include: Customer, Test, Developers, Operational, Help Desk, Engineering, CM, Program Management, and Approval Board.

Established Release

Using the UDS model is built around releasing quality software. Software requirements are defined in and identified for a targeted release. Components are gathered in the UDS model process as well as maintenance requirements.

Establishment of Release Target

USER-DEFINED SOFTWARE

This baseline depends on the addition of new capabilities which could be release independent of defects. However, the release target for maintenance is to include those items in small portions of software identified for repair.

Maintain Version Control

Version control is critical for the configuration control. A CM tool is extremely important in the total process to maintain proper configuration and release of the products. Product version is typically equal to a Configuration Item and can be tracked accordingly.

Release Baseline

The release baseline is based on the product being released to production to include the total product and all associated documentation. It is important for a Configuration Audit as the product is moved through the different developments identified in Annex C-Types of Environments.

Application Baseline

The application baseline is critical to maintain continuity throughout the UDS model.

Database Baseline

The database baseline is likewise critical for the UDS model to maintain and ensure the total system and all the components are maintained and managed.

Add other paragraphs as needed to ensure the configuration is maintained and the software meets quality and total user functionality.

USER-DEFINED SOFTWARE

TEST PLANNING

Delivery of software is tedious work, especially for the Configuration Manager to capture the right code with the right version. Continuously delivery of software is a well within the realms of possibility and does have some validity in large ecosystems. However, such a venture is not without risk. Delivery of software within the UDS model is based on user interaction with the product and stakeholder to ensure acceptance.

Applying a continuous model for delivery of software bears risk, unless in a very closed and secure ecosystem. Creating the automation for the testing of a product is a challenge within itself. Maintenance of the continuous delivery tool is also a tedious task but overtime the team will adapt to the tool. Think in terms of the repetition rules where over time doing the same event improves speed and thus throughput.

Small maintenance release require regression testing to ensure the change is system compatible. If this case an automated test tool is invaluable, simply to make sure the change is compatible with the total system.

Continuous delivery implies automated testing in most cases. However, automated testing is truthfully <u>not</u> a panacea from a test perspective. Testing is at the heart of the UDS model. Automated testing can serve as the need for larger bulk driven testing such as performance testing, system testing, and end-to-end testing. Automated testing has its place in the future of software development, but it comes with a cost.

USER-DEFINED SOFTWARE

Automated testing has its place specifically where regression testing is needed. But automated testing can be a hindrance for small maintenance release. Automated testing can serve the needs for a larger release, but it requires **DEDICATED** developers to maintain the automated tool. A front-end user might be able to keep the tool up to date, but the best solution is to have technical test tool experts as part of the UDS team. Their longevity is just as valuable as other team members.

The UDS model favors careful test planning and test documentation over lengthy system level documentation and narratives. A good test plan will capture the needed elements for the system, business rules, data properties for the entity relation diagram (ERD}, database relational designs etc.

All test scripts will address the user needs, from the input requirements-to-the outputs either displayed on the screen or printed material.

This site provides a list of top-rated test tools. However, over time this list may become obsolete. (Top 20 Best Automation Testing Tools in 2019 (Comprehensive List), www.softwaretestinghelp.com/top-20-automation-testing-tools

When assessing the pros and cons for suggest reading 10 Best Test Automated Strategies and Practices: (10 Best Test Automation Strategies And Practices: https://www.softwaretestinghelp.com/automation-testing-tutorial-7/)

Keep manual testing needs separate from the automated testing. These two elements must be kept separate and apart. The experience level is the key for this separation,

Allow the users to set the test scenarios from the UCM. They will determine the appropriate test scenarios along with the test parameters.

TEST PLAN EXAMPLE

TEST PLAN

For

Template Example

dd/mm/yyyy

Name _____
Project Test Manager

Name_____
Program Manager

Name_____
Lead Engineer

Name_____
Customer (Acknowledgement)

TABLE OF CONTENTS

Build the table of content to the UDS team's own unique specifications.

REVISION HISTORY & SIGN-OFF SHEET

Design a document for managing the revisions.

USER-DEFINED SOFTWARE

CHANGE RECORD

Use to show the changes once the document is baselined.

REVIEWERS

List the reviews

DISTRIBUTION

List recipients the document

DOCUMENT PROPERTIES

Provide document history and revision.

INTRODUCTION

The purpose of this document is to outline the UDS testing process for the project. Approval of this document implies that reviewers are confident that following the execution of the test plan, the resulting system will be considered fully tested and eligible for implementation.

UDS testing team completes testing the software. The testing is conducted to enable a user to validate that the software meets the agreed upon acceptance criteria.

PROJECT OVERVIEW

Describe the effort in this section.

SCOPE

In Scope - Scope is used to bound the work.

USER-DEFINED SOFTWARE

Out of Scope - Keep in mind scope creep can occur so list areas not relevant to scope of the project.

OBJECTIVE

Primary Objective

UDS Test team conducts testing to ensure that the system satisfies **the needs** of the business as specified in the needs statement and requirements and provides confidence in its use. Modifications to the requirements will be captured and tested to the highest level of quality. NO SOFTWARE BEFORE ITS TIME means don't release broken software.

Additional Objective

To identify and expose defects and associated risks, communicate all known issues to the project team, and ensure that all issues are addressed in an appropriate manner prior to implementation.

UDS TEST METHODOLOGY

Address the testing activities such as automated and/or manual testing.

Automated tests have their place in testing, especially for functionality testing. However, hand-on testing is the key to gaining an appreciation from the front-line user's perspective.

UDS Test team conducts the test (i.e., front-line, functional (Subject Matter Experts) and Corporate Stakeholders). Users will execute all test scripts referenced in the testing activities. Users may also perform additional tests not detailed in the plan but remain relevant and within the scope of the project. The test manager tracks the progress and reports progress.

TEST PHASES

Outline specific test phases.

UDS TEST ENVIRONMENT

Document the test environments. For instance, if the testing is conducted within the staging environment for changing environment.

Applicable IP addresses and URLs should be provided to the UDS Team and all workstations should be configured appropriately for access to the test environment.

UDS TEST DESKTOPS

Each test participant will have a desktop or device exactly like the one within the field. Notes on device usage are appropriate, along with any special instructions for conducting the test.

UDS TEST DATA

Test data and test database synchronization is an essential element in the testing, along with resetting the SYSTEM CLOCKS. Test data in many situations is time sensitive, for instance in financial payments for prompt payment process. The wrong system clock and a test database must be reset for subsequent test. It is of NO value to rerun test scripts into a test database a second time unless the original parameters are set. Therefore, documentation of the time stamp for the database, version, test scripts etc, is crucial.

USER-DEFINED SOFTWARE

Access to test data is a vital component in conducting a comprehensive test of the system. All UDS participants will require usage of test accounts and other pertinent test data which should be provided by end user support upon request. Participants not currently utilizing test data must receive appropriate clearance and/or permissions to perform desired actions in the UDS test environment. All user roles should fully emulate production path/test accounts.

UDS TEST ROLES AND RESPONSIBILITIES

Keys to a successful UDS test process involve open channels of communication, detailed documentation, and above all, clearly defined roles and responsibilities. Each team member must function fluidly in a UDS group setting as well as work independently for extended periods of time. UDS testing is a collaborative test process. UDS team analyzes the test results from different perspectives with various levels of expertise across the needs to ensure success.

UDS TEST TEAM

The test team is comprised of members from the test team who possess a thorough knowledge of the current systems and processing methods. These team members will be better able to initiate test input, review the results, and be more intuitively familiar with the impact on other related business issues and staff activities.

Test team roles vary, with the fundamental purpose to test the total capability and functionality.

UDS INTERFACE TEST PARTNERS

USER-DEFINED SOFTWARE

In a major release of software of even a maintenance release, having interface test partners identified and available for testing will ensure success.

UDS DELIVERABLES

The following sections detail milestones crucial to the completion of the UDS phase of the project. Once all dependent milestones have been completed, UDS will formally sign-off on the system's functionality and distribute an e-mail to all project stakeholders.

use.

TEST SCHEDULE

A planned schedule is sometimes needed, especially in a large extensive effort. A plan is important in this case.

UDS TEST CASES

Test cases provide a high-level description of the functionality to be tested. All regression and new functionality test cases are contained in the Use Case Model (UCM) for example. However, capturing them in other automated test tools is important to ensure comprehensive testing. The team should plan to leverage relevant test cases for project specific functionality. Each UDS test case must reference a specific functional requirement. Remember this golden rule: <u>If a requirement is not testable then the requirement is not valid.</u>

Test cases contain a detailed step by step breakdown of each test case to be performed by the UDS tester. Each script contains: Project and Project ID, Release ID if available, test case number, product, test description, requirement number, requestor, tester, action to be performed, test data to be utilized, expected results, error descriptions (if applicable), pass/fail results, date tested, and any additional comments from the UDS tester.

Maximize automated testing. Document the tool and storage location of test data and scripts.

Automated testing output is a source for validation and verification of successful testing.

Keep a **Requirement Traceability Matrix (RTM)** and track it to the test scripts and test scenarios.

A spreadsheet is an excellent tool for maintaining the RTM.

UDS TEST DEFECTS

UDS team documents the release defects and the Test Manager tracks the defects back through the system for repair. The defect is recycled back into maintenance process. Since the defect is part of a release, a release defect has a higher priority than field defects in maintenance. A release defect is reworked until fixed, because it has stopped the release. Each entry will include detailed information about each defect.

UDS DEFECT TRACKING

Team members will be provided with instruction on how to effectively execute test scripts, as well identify, capture, and report defects. Team members present finding findings on regularly scheduled team meetings. Testers provide details of the test, along with expected outputs versus the actual test outputs.

DEFECT PROBLEM IDENTIFICATION

USER-DEFINED SOFTWARE

The CRIT problem resolution diagram is an excellent tool for problem analysis.

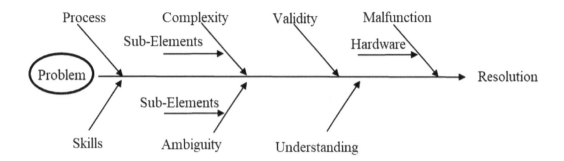

Defects must be clearly captured and escalated to ensure prompt resolution by development.

RISK

Below are risks that could potentially impact the testing process and prevent its successful and timely completion:

> ➤ Unstable test environment.
> ➤ Inadequate test data.
> ➤ Incorrect software version(s).
> ➤ Failure to emulate production environment.

ASSUMPTIONS

Add assumptions as appropriate. Below please find a couple of examples:

Configuration information and test data has been provided and applied as designed.

UDS test team is available to participate in testing.

USER-DEFINED SOFTWARE

REFERENCES

List as needed.

GLOSSARY

Define as needed. Basic Definition for the Test Plan:

Identify UDS Team – Numerous members of the UDS test team will be part of the testing activities.

UDS Plan – A strategy-based document defining test methodology and criteria is distributed to the team.

UDS Plan Team Review – Session with business stakeholders to review plan and provide feedback and sign-off.

UDS Test Cases – A document that details each specific test case that will be performed during the UDS process.

UDS Test Data – Receipt of accounts and test environment data is required to execute test scripts. *Note: Plan for the lead time to get proper test accounts.*

UDS Test Cases – A detailed step-by-step breakdown of each individual test case.

UDS Test Case Review – Approval from business team and/or third parties on completed scripts.

UDS Desktop Validation – Validation of installed applications and configuration necessary for testing.

UDS Environment Validation – Validation of connectivity and expected results in the test environment for each end user participating in testing.

UDS Test Case Execution – Completion of all test scripts by test team.

UDS Defect Tracking – Defects will be entered and tracked via spreadsheet by the Business Analyst and/or Project Manager. Each entry will include detailed information about each defect.

UDS Touch Point – Regularly scheduled meeting to evaluate UDS progress and outstanding defects.

UDS Sign-Off – Formal sign-off indicating the system satisfies the needs of the business as specified in the functional requirements and provides confidence in its

ANNEX B – TESTING STEPS

UDS TESTING

UDS testing is not much different than traditional testing activities with the exception it has the User as a very interactive part of development testing. The technical team (coder and database expertise) are active in the change testing process for code changes; however, the user is actively involved. The user is an integral part of the UDS development in the increment

Iteration Testing

Iteration Testing is the start of the testing activities where the Front-Line User is highly interactive in the development of the product. The technical team is equally involved in the testing as each piece of functionality is added. The individual units are tested by the developers, and, correspondingly, once they have a product, the Front-Line user test the product also. Their testing is to ensure the product is producing the right results/meeting expectations and functionality. At this point in time the technical writer is engaged to document the testing. If an automated test tool is part of the development and delivery, which it should be, then began to configure the tool as the product is built.

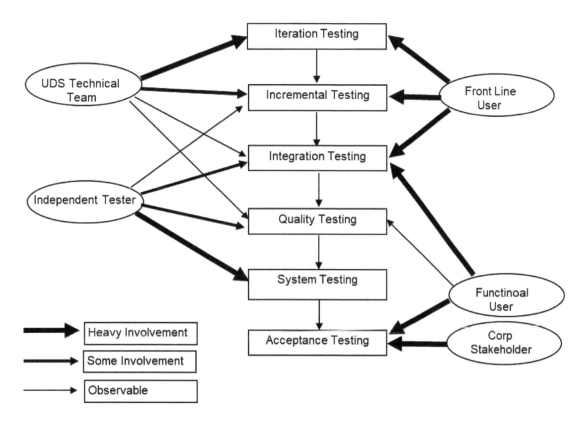

Figure Annex B 1.0 UDS Testing

Remember the goal of the iteration is the development of a specific portion of a component through the 2-week work package. Continue adding the WBS-02 items to the component until the component is complete and the Front-Line User agrees to the component.

USER-DEFINED SOFTWARE

Incremental Testing:

A product will contain more than one component unless it is a maintenance release. Even then the increment will most likely include more than one iteration. The UDS team continues to add components as Iteration until the product is ready for promoting to Increment Testing. The incremental primary test is conducted by the Front-Line User. If an automated test tool is used, then it is used to conduct the test. The output is verified by the Front-Line User. If an error is discovered, then the product is looped back into an iteration for repair. It is highly possible that the error can be included in a pending iteration and brought through the process. On the other hand, depending on the gravity of the error a separate iteration may be started to repair the defect.

Incremental builds are continued as part of the UDS model with the intention of adding components until the WBS-01 is complete. Since more than one WBS-01 is part of the product, each WBS-01 is tested independently until each is agreed to be completed by the user.

Integration Testing:

Integration Test is combining all the WBS-01 into a completed package. The testing from an Integration serves two purposes. (First) Integration Testing is to ensure incremental conformity to ensure the increments meet form and fit. In other words, the links work, transfer of data occurs, and one increment doesn't break another. (Second) Integration Testing is a functional test. The test team is expanded to include a second set of users who will also test the product against the functionality to prove the functional aspect of the product under consideration. It is this testing that will incorporate the same actions in the iteration testing but goes beyond the mere aspects of testing the component into the testing of the total product in the planned release into production.

Quality Testing:

Quality testing is the testing accomplished by an independent test team as a check of the product to ensure the product is meeting total expectations prior to turning over the product for other testing especially Acceptance Testing. Quality testing is End-to-End testing to ensure there are no errors in the planned software as well as to check the operability with the Operating System from a compatibility perspective.

System Testing:

System Testing is defined for our purposes as encompassing performance and load balance testing but is not part of the UDS model. However, system testing in some software releases is essential due to the size of the product, as well as the critical nature of the work being performed by the system.

Acceptance Testing: **Testing**

Acceptance Testing is accomplished by a separate group of users, such as Corporate Stakeholders or with additional functional users. Acceptance testing is the last check of the product to ensure the functionality from end-to-end and is done from a user's focus perspective. The acceptance testing will be signed off by the Customer of the product. This artifact will be used as the authority to release the product into production.

ANNEX C - TYPES OF ENVIRONMENTS

The UDS model discusses these four different environments: Development, Integration, Acceptance and Production. These environments must be kept in synchronous status to include the Operating System, Database, Application Code and tool set. Version control is extremely critical to ensure continuity of the software. Configuration Manager is the most critical resource in maintaining configuration management of all environments.

Also, the hardware configuration in all these environments must be the same for the CPU, memory. Disk capacity is important simply to ensure space is not strained. Capacity of the Development Environment may be less than the remaining three platforms. However, the Integration Environment needs to match the Production Environment in total. This is necessary to ensure any load testing of the software will perform with exactness in Production. Load testing, while not discussed as part of the UDS model can occur as part of Integration Testing based on the magnitude of the software release. Load testing is most beneficial under certain situations with a high volume of transactions.

Acceptance Environment may equal the Development Environment, since the purpose of the acceptance activities is to test the functionality of the code. However, there must be enough capacity for normal response for the users during their testing activities.

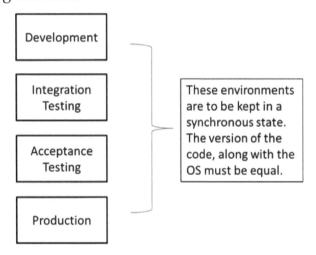

USER-DEFINED SOFTWARE

```
┌─────────────┐
│   Staging   │
└─────────────┘
┌───────────────────────────────┐
│ - This environment is used for │
│ new version capabilities released │
│ by a Vendor, such as the OS.   │
│                                │
│ - The test environment is loaded │
│ on the Staging environment to  │
│ test the system from end-to-end. │
│                                │
│ - At a designated time, the    │
│ Development Environment will    │
│ be frozen as a Base Line, loaded │
│ on staging for a final test.   │
│                                │
│ - Once Base Line passes, then  │
│ other environments will be     │
│ loaded.                        │
└───────────────────────────────┘
```

Annex C 1.0 Test Environments

The Staging Environment is a special environment necessary to test the system for new versions. The capacity of the Staging Environment will eventually need to be comparable to the Production. Once the software is fully tested, appropriate application code is developed, then a full performance test is needed to ensure the new version will not break the system.

ANNEX D – FRAMEWORKS and METHODOLOGY

There are several software development frameworks and methodologies. Twelve are outlined by Acodez which provides for a description of each along with the Pros and Cons of each.[26] Use this reference to preview the various software development models.

Let's take a look at two models from a historical perspective: Waterfall and Spiral models respective.

---

[26] Acodez, 12 BEST SOFTWARE DEVELOPMENT METHODOLOGIES WITH PROS AND CONS, June, 01, 2018, https://acodez.in/12-best-software-development-methodologies-pros-cons/

WATERFALL MODEL

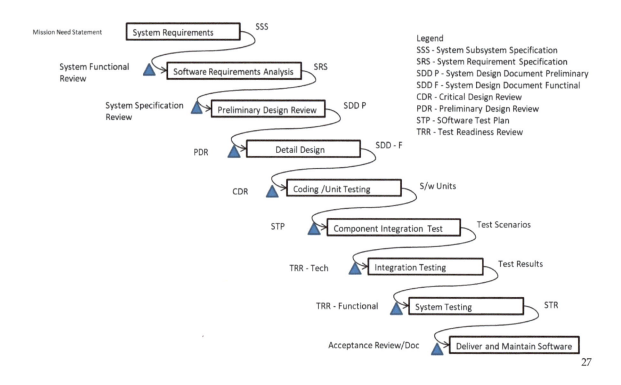

Figure Annex D 1 – Waterfall Model

In the Waterfall Model notice the addition of the elaborate documentation required at the beginning and end of the phases as the model progress. This elaborate documentation became a burden in the delivery of a product on time.

Next, is the Spiral model which began the slow migration away from the Waterfall Model.

---

[27] Waterfall Model with Documentation, Software Workshop, HOFF Industries 2015

SPRAL MODEL

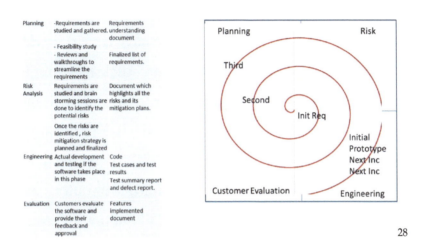

28

Figure Annex D 2 – Spiral Model

SCRUM FRAMEWORK

SCRUM emerged as popular framework. "The Scrum framework consists of Scrum Teams and their associated roles, events, artifacts, and rules. Each component within the framework serves a specific purpose and is essential to Scrum's success and usage. The rules of Scrum bind together the roles, events, and artifacts, governing the relationships and interaction between them." [29]

---

[28] Software Testing Help, Spiral Model – What Is SDLC Spiral Model?
August 21, 2019, https://www.softwaretestinghelp.com/spiral-model-what-is-sdlc-spiral-model/

[29] Ken Schwaber and Jeff Sutherland, "The Scrum Guide™", November 2017,
https://www.scrumguides.org/ .

USER-DEFINED SOFTWARE

The problems in the history of software development were three-fold: (1) Cost Overruns from missed schedules, which added more the total cost of ownership; (2) Poor delivery of missed requirements; (3) User accepting a product they did not concur but was compelled to take due to their desires for a product.

A change was evident when two new terms began to have a solid foundation in software development: iterative and incremental in an article by Craig Larman in 2003.[30] Further, in the 1985 DOD-STD-2167 in section 4.1.2 identified these two terms. These terms, for software development methods, were contrary to the traditional models, but their value became critical in improving the delivery of software. It became evident during development; multiple iterations may be in progress at the same time. Evolutionary or incremental build grew from this approach. In software, the relationship between iterations and increments is determined by the overall software development process.

Two other models Evolutionary and Extreme Programming[31] began to take shape in industries, which were in instrumental in establishing the UDS 4-D's Model

UDS FRAMEWORK AND MODELS

However, the UDS origins stem from the **4-D's Development** model seen below, which first started in 2005. The value of the 4-D's model realized the Waterfall Model concentrated on documentation and very little on the actual development

---

[30] Larman, Craig (June 2003). "Iterative and Incremental Development: A Brief History", Computer, p36 (6): 47–56.).
[31] Blueprint, https://www.blueprintsys.com/agile-development-101/agile-methodologies

of the code, coupled with the time box of a schedule to meet the deliverable product. Quality seemed to be less critical, and the USER was non-existent in the development process. Delivery of a product based on schedule was more important than quality and meeting user expectations.

The UDS model today has not changed in detail except adding the user throughout the process. The model has flavors of the 12 Methods listed at the start of this Anne, because when analyzing the other methodologies and their development processes, they all seemingly have a favorable attribute but lack uniformity in the delivery of a product.

The UDS model supports the AGILE Manifesto introduced in 2001[32] with the idea of a product over process which is indeed a positive step. Early in the history of the development of Agile, the developer struggled with the problem of substantial weighted documentation. But, the development of software must be driven by a purpose.

From The Agile Manifesto the following sets the tone for their framework used today:

"We are uncovering better ways of developing software by doing it and helping others do it. Through this work we have come to value:

Individuals and interactions	over	processes and tools
Working software	over	comprehensive documentation
Customer collaboration	over	contract negotiation
Responding to change	over	following a plan.

---

[32] Kent Beck, et al, "Manifesto for Agile Software Development", 2001, https://agilemanifesto.org/

That is, while there is value in the items on the right, we value the items on the left more"[33]

"These 12 Principles are at the heart of the Agile Methodology:

1. Customer satisfaction by rapid delivery of useful software
2. Welcome changing requirements, even late in development
3. Working software is delivered frequently (weeks rather than months)
4. Working software is the principal measure of progress
5. Sustainable development, able to maintain a constant pace
6. Close, daily cooperation between business people and developers
7. Face-to-face conversation is the best form of communication (co-location)
8. Projects are built around motivated individuals, who should be trusted
9. Continuous attention to technical excellence and good design
10. Simplicity—the art of maximizing the amount of work not done—is essential
11. Self-organizing teams
12. Regular adaptation to changing circumstances"[34]

CURRENT UDS 4-D's MODEL

The current UDS model from its origins has not changed drastically over the years, except for user interaction throughout the model. In all development activities, the fundamental theme for developing software remains the same from the inception of the Waterfall model. Requirements Design, Development, Testing, and Delivery are all fundamentally the same. The UDS model does these steps in short small deliveries with the user concurrence throughout the entire

[33] Ibid
[34] Ibid

process.

The UDS team is interactive in every phase of the model and therefore included throughout the development.

Both New Capabilities and Maintenance follow these same steps. The degree of the release is dependent on the work performed. Users and stakeholders often propose the idea of a partial software release for a new capability. Releasing part of a new capability has many dependencies, but it is highly possible and is a joint decision between the product owner and the UDS team.

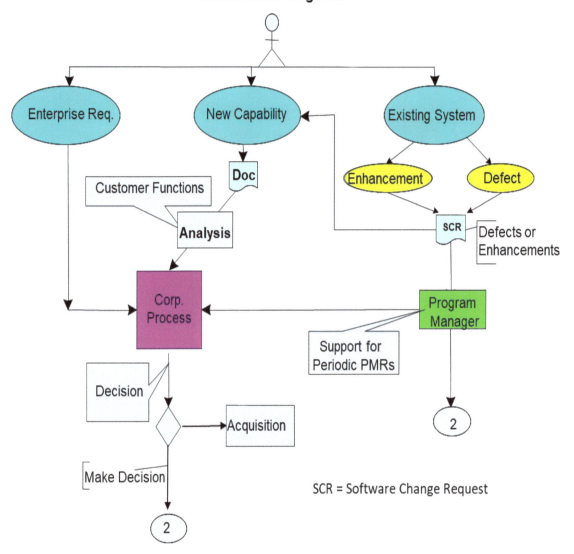

Figure Annex D 3 Part 1: 4-D's

Notice the top levels of the model conforms to the need's assessments explained in Chapter 4. The are fundamental sources for where needs occur in software.

4 Ds Development Processes

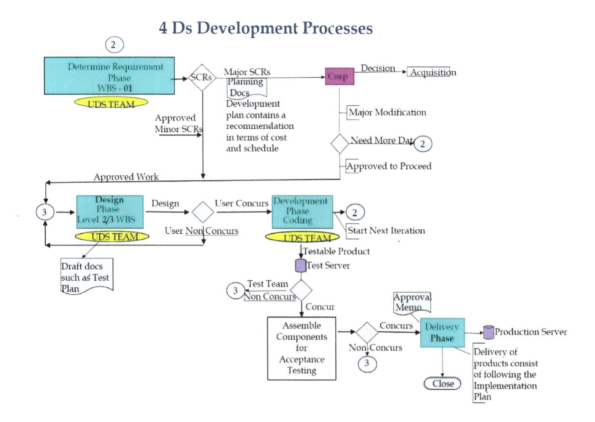

Figure Annex D 4 Part 2: 4-D's

UDS 4-D's is an iterative and incremental approach to the development of the software per chapters in this book. It is important to recap the model once again to reinforce the concepts of iterations containing components.

Incremental approach to add functionality via iterations for adding/building **components**

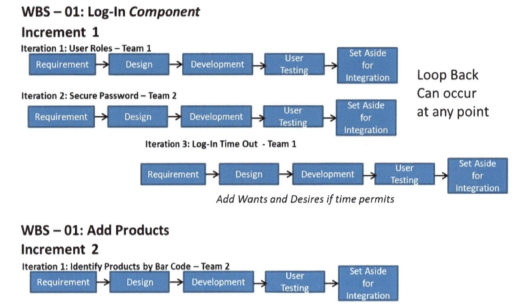

Figure Annex D 5 – UDS Increments

Notice WBS -01 for the Log-In Component contains Increments which contain the Iterations. These iterations are small portions of work, related to a spiral labeled Two Week work packages.

The total model includes the extensive testing and integrations.

Figure Annex D 6 – UDS Merger

USER-DEFINED SOFTWARE

Figure Annex D 7 – UDS Testing

All the frameworks and methods have a certain place and the decision as to which one to use is purely subjective.

All methods have good intention in the delivery of quality software but most of the overruns came from the sheer assumption that developers knew what the user wanted. This is a fundamental failure to assume requirements are known when they aren't, but requirements can come to life when the developers/engineers join in discussion and dialog with the users. This is an essential ingredient in the quality process for software development and the delivery of software that meets customer expectations and quality.

Developing software for the past eons was built with the mindset that software to be built requires a rigorous upfront surge of interaction and focus on desk application so as to write a good software specification and then have a developer come in or better yet build a product based on what the customer thought they wrote and what the developer thought they read. The seriousness of the problem that consistently faced software developers using old methods was halfway through the development the users says the dreaded two words – "you know', 'I forgot', "I missed' etc. Either way those comments sent a signal immediately that something else is coming and it could have a major impact on cost and schedule.

USER-DEFINED SOFTWARE

The UDS Model is the only User-Oriented Model.

Requirements>Properties> Criteria > Complexity>Iteration

Iterations>Increments> Components >Products>Capabilities>Systems

UDS = User-Oriented Software Development and Delivery Model

ANNEX E - USE CASE MODELING (UCM)

SHORT GUIDE - USE CASE MODEL

USE CASE origination began in 1986 when Ivar Jacobson used visual diagrams to depict users in their roles in a business model.[35]

A use case documents how a user interacts with an information system. Use cases are written to support the main purpose for a component and system. Use Cases documents the main scenarios and alternative scenarios.

Below is a sample UCM to derive user's requirements. There are several modeling techniques such as the Use Case techniques in the reference above

---

[35]Ivar Jacobson, *Object-Oriented Software Engineering - A Use Case Driven Approach 1st Edition*, Addison-Wesley, 1992.

Object-Oriented Software Engineering. Historically, Unified Modeling Language (UML)[36] took the center stage for software model visualization. The reemergence of visual modeling, in lieu of lengthy word pictures is taking center stage in software development.

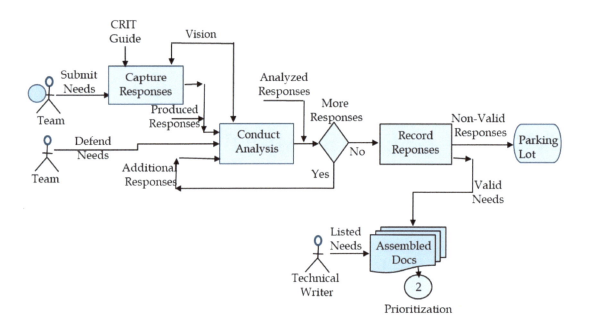

Figure Annex E.1 Use Case Model

(Note: Technical Writer in figure E.1 is included in the system area for exposition only due to space limitations. Tools are not included due to space. Drivers begin outside the system boundary.)

USE CASE MODELING BENEFITS

Use cases modeling provides the pictorial view that enable a faster visualization of the process. This doesn't mean the details per Chapter 5 are in pictures, but the

---

[36]Unified Modeling Language, https://www.uml.org/

details are written in the documents. The facilitator, UDS team, Technical Writer, Test Developer all work together to develop software within the model. The UDS format supports the Agile process but enables the team to follow a defined process for the creation of the software.

While documentation does occur, it is **not** a long, drawn out process at the beginning of the project, as in the early days of software development. A technical writer documents the concepts, ideas, etc. as they occur, which is an important part of the model development. Having a test developer is a key ingredient for quality software. <u>Modeling is an excellent technique to produce ideas and general information about requirements from all users.</u>

UCM has several advantages. UCM bring the following five terms into focus for the software development.

<u>Need >Requirements>Components>Properties>Criteria</u>

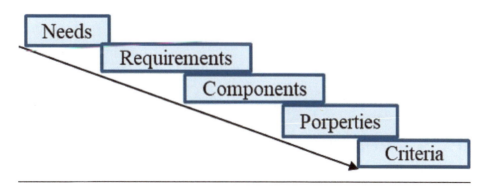

Figure Annex E.2 UDS Flow Diagram

➢ UCM advances the design,

- ➤ UCM provides visual depiction,

- ➤ UCM supports estimating, scheduling, and validating effort,

- ➤ UCM are reusable within a project,

- ➤ UCM supports staging of increments and working with priorities.,

- ➤ UCM support the iteration, iterative, component and system development,

- ➤ UCM enable business rules visualization and testing,

- ➤ UCM focuses on interactions between the user and the system,

- ➤ UCM enables visually seeing out-bound and in-bound interfaces,

- ➤ UCM visually prepares releases, enabling adding or removing component,

- ➤ UCM models become part of the life cycle documentation.

The details required for software development are in the WBS and definitions of what the user needs. UCMs serve a valuable purpose to help with the WBS. However, none of these will eliminate the need for a close working relationship with the using community and developers.

USE CASE MODELING PURPOSES

The overall purpose is to deliver quality products wanted by the users.

Each UCM focuses on describing how to achieve a single business rule or goal/task. It is best to let the UDS team work on one component and its intricacies using UCM techniques. Many layers and multiple UCMs are necessary to achieve the goals.

Actors are parties outside the system that interact with the system; an actor can be any of the 3 levels of users described in this document: Front-Line User,

USER-DEFINED SOFTWARE

Functional User, Corporate User, and their specific roles users in their interactions with the system.

UCM has two important purposes:

> ➤ The first visual identification of requirements,
> ➤ The second purpose is interactions of the UDS team.

USE CASE MODELING GOALS

> ➤ Provide a visual description of the product,
> ➤ Limit elaborate wordy documentation,
> ➤ Meet cost objective with quality software,
> ➤ Reduce recycle time,
> ➤ Reduce fielded errors.

GENERAL INFORMATION

1) There is no set template. However, the documents referenced in this Annex provide useful insight.

2) Several important UCM considerations: Naming convention, version, date, definitions, actors, team, notes, business rules, guidance/laws, interfaces, scope, association with other UCMs, interfaces, inbound and outbound triggers, and relationship in the system.

USER-DEFINED SOFTWARE

UDS USE CASE MODEL

UDS understands the history of Inputs and Outputs as terms in information technology and modeling. Also, the frequent use of the term Activity. However, those terms lacked enough fidelity to clearly explain the intentions. Simply using Activity as a descriptor failed to capture the actual work accomplished. Similarly, the input term failed to adequately communicate the items used to start the work endeavor. UDS favors using DRIVER as the term to deliver materials and non-materials into the work effort.

The key element for the UDS models is the WORK function, therefore, the purpose of the model is to describe the work. The intention of using WORK in the UDS model is to ensure the effort produces a product. Production of work is the true purpose of the functions, else, there is no value to the function. Unless the work produces a product, then the question of value becomes a question even to the point of deleting the work function. Lastly, the work must have productivity in the form of PRODUCTION from work performed.

Notice the UDS Work Model below where the focus in the work performed. The drivers are identified as either material or non-non-material entering the work effort. The end state of the work effort is the production of a product. The model's goal is to define the work effort to produce a product, even if the product is used in other work efforts. The ultimate goal is a product for use and acceptable to the customers and stakeholders.

USER-DEFINED SOFTWARE

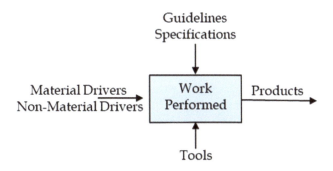

Figure Annex E.3 – UDS Work Model

ANNEX F - DEFINITIONS

Unless otherwise indicated below the definition within this annex all stems came from one source: https://csrc.nist.gov/glossary?index=P

Acceptance – The criteria necessary for both the user and customer (Acceptance Members) to concur on the product.

Adaptive Maintenance - Concerned with the change in the software that takes place to make the software adaptable to new environment such as to run the software on a new operating system. Dinesh Thakur, Types of Software Maintenance, ECOMPUTER NOTES, http://ecomputernotes.com/software-engineering/types-of-software-maintenance

USER-DEFINED SOFTWARE

Attribute - An attribute is any distinctive feature, characteristic, or property of an object that can be identified or isolated quantitatively or qualitatively by either human or automated means. In *computing*, an *attribute* is a specification that defines a property of an object, element, or file. It may also refer to or set the specific value for a given instance of such. For clarity, *attributes* should more correctly be considered metadata.

Backlog – The work remaining to be accomplished regardless of industry.

Capability Owner – The entity who will own the capability.

Configuration - The possible conditions, parameters, and specifications with which an information system or system component can be described or arranged.

Configuration item - An entity [Iteration/Increment] within a configuration that satisfies an end use IT function and that can be uniquely identified at a given reference point.

Corrective maintenance - Reactive modification of a software product performed after delivery to correct discovered faults. Dinesh Thakur, Types of Software Maintenance, ECOMPUTER NOTES, http://ecomputernotes.com/software-engineering/types-of-software-maintenance

Customer – Is the actual purchaser of the product; one that purchases a commodity or service. Regardless if the development is for software, building, etc. [Equals Capability Owner]. https://www.merriam-webster.com/dictionary/customer

USER-DEFINED SOFTWARE

Database Expert – The person or persons with expertise in the database structures.

Decomposition - Separate into constituent parts or elements or into simpler compounds.

Done – In Information Technology error free software accepted by both the user and customer; User-Defined Software, Hoff Industries, 2019.

Driver – The material and Non-Material elements to drive work for the production of a product.

Emergency - Unscheduled corrective maintenance/release performed to keep a system operational.

Enhancement - To increase or improve in value, quality, desirability, or attractiveness. https://www.merriam-webster.com/dictionary/enhancement

Enterprise - A systematic purposeful activity; a unit of or activity. https://www.merriam-webster.com/dictionary/enterprise

Entity - An individual (person), organization, device or process. It is perfectly acceptable to consider an entity as another system, where an interface or linkage to the system (1 way or 2 ways) exist.

Entity Relationship Diagram – A diagram showing relationships with a database structure. In a relational database the primary and foreign keys are identied.

USER-DEFINED SOFTWARE

Functional - Designed or developed chiefly from the point of view of the user.
https://www.merriam-webster.com/dictionary/functional

Functional Testing - Testing that verifies that an implementation of some function operates correctly.

Implementation – The functions needed to deliver the capability or product.

Interface - Common boundary between independent systems or modules where interactions take place.

Maintenance - Any act that either prevents the failure or malfunction of equipment/software or restores its operating capability.

Model – Depiction of the users' process leading to the creation of requirements for software development.

Need - A lack of something requisite, desirable, or useful; a condition requiring supply or relief. https://www.merriam-webster.com/dictionary/need

Object - Passive information system-related entity (e.g., devices, files, records, tables, processes, programs, domains) containing or receiving information. Access to an object (by a subject) implies access to the information it contains.

Perfective maintenance - Modification of an IT product after deliver to improve performance or maintainability. Dinesh Thakur, Types of Software Maintenance,

USER-DEFINED SOFTWARE

ECOMPUTER NOTES, http://ecomputernotes.com/software-engineering/types-of-software-maintenance

Preventative Maintenance - Involves implementing changes to prevent the occurrence of errors. Dinesh Thakur, Types of Software Maintenance, ECOMPUTER NOTES, http://ecomputernotes.com/software-engineering/types-of-software-maintenance

Process - A set of interrelated activities, which transforms inputs into outputs

Product – The results from working, that which is achieved through mental, physical human, machine effort or digital manipulation.

Product Owner – Is the entity that owns the product either a material product or non-material in terms of data, intellectual and technical rights.

Property - The property of being genuine and being able to be verified and trusted; confidence in the validity of a transmission. The *property* may be considered a form of object in its own right, able to possess other *properties*.

Release - A particular version of a configuration item that is made available for a specific purpose. A collection of new and/or changed configuration items which are tested and introduced into a production environment together.

Requirement - A condition or capability that must be met or possessed by a system or system element to satisfy a contract, standard, specification, or other formally imposed documents.

USER-DEFINED SOFTWARE

Requirement Traceability Matrix – A technique to trace requirements through testing with an identification process.

Scrum (N) - A framework within which people can address complex adaptive problems, while productively and creatively delivering products of the highest possible value. https://www.scrumguides.org/docs/scrumguide/v2017/2017-Scrum-Guide-US.pdf#zoom=100 .

Software - "Organized information in the form of operating systems, utilities, programs, and applications that enable computers to work. Software consists of carefully organized instructions and code written by programmers in any of various special computer languages. Software is divided commonly into two main categories: (1) System software: controls the basic (and invisible to the user) functions of a computer and comes usually preinstalled with the machine. See also BIOS and Operating System. (2) Application software: handles multitudes of common and specialized tasks a user wants to perform, such as accounting, communicating, data processing, word processing."
Source: http://www.businessdictionary.com/definition/software.html

Software Component - Parts of a system or application. Components are a means of breaking the complexity of software into manageable parts.

Software/System Engineer - A branch of computer science that deals with the design, implementation, and maintenance of complex computer programs.
https://www.merriam-webster.com/dictionary/software%20engineer

USER-DEFINED SOFTWARE

Software Pocket Factory – A location of experts dedicated to the delivery of a single component or a unified capability; User-Defined Software, Hoff Industries, 2019.

Source Code - A computer program in its original programming language (such as FORTRAN or C) before translation into object code usually by a compiler. https://www.merriam-webster.com/dictionary/source%20code

Stakeholder - Individual or organization having a right, share, claim, or interest in a system or in its possession of characteristics that meet their needs and expectations.

System - (A) A set of interlinked units organized to accomplish one or several specific functions. (B) An integrated composite that consists of one or more of the processes, hardware, software, facilities and people, that provides a capability to satisfy a stated need or objective.

System Analysis - The act, process, or profession of studying an activity (such as a procedure, a business, or a physiological function) typically by mathematical means in order to define its goals or purposes and to discover operations and procedures for accomplishing them most efficiently. https://www.merriam-webster.com/dictionary/systems%20analyses

Technical Writer – The entity responsible for the documentation of the teams work.

Test Developer/Engineer – Leading software expertise responsible for the automated testing functions.

UDS Facilitator/Lead – The person who will guide the effort to deliver a quality product.

User – Actual person/entity who uses the result of the development. They have a special interest in the product. An entity could be another software system that receive the data thus it would be a user or consumer of the data. Individual or group that interacts with a system or benefits from a system during its utilization.

Validation - Confirmation by examination and provision of objective evidence that the particular requirements for a specific intended use are fulfilled.

Version - (A) An identified instance of an item. (B) Modification to a version of a software product, resulting in a new version, requires configuration management action.

Work – The actions, physical or mental for producing or creation of a product or a result.

BIBLIOGRAPHY

Acodez, *12 BEST SOFTWARE DEVELOPMENT METHODOLOGIES WITH PROS AND CONS*, June 01, 2018, https://acodez.in/12-best-software-development-methodologies-pros-cons/

Anderson, David J., Kanban: Successfully Evolutionary Change for your Technology Business, 2010, https://www.digite.com/kanban/what-is-kanban/

Beck, Kent, et al, *Manifesto for Agile Software Development*, 2001, https://agilemanifesto.org/

Blueprint, https://www.blueprintsys.com/agile-development-101/agile-methodologies

Bridges, Jennifer, *What Is a Work Breakdown Structure?* Project Manager, June 3, 2014, https://www.projectmanager.com/training/what-is-a-work-breakdown-structure

Business Dictionary, Definitions, http://www.businessdictionary.com/definition/software.html

Chau, Celestine, *Law of Diminishing Returns,* Personal Excellence, https://personalexcellence.co/blog/law-of-diminishing-returns/

Cheylene T., *How to Classify Bug Severity in Your Bug Report*, LEAN TESTING, 2005, https://leantesting.com/how-to-classify-bug-severity/

ECOMPUTER NOTES, http://ecomputernotes.com/software-engineering/types-of-software-maintenance

Gitt, Werner, *Scientific laws of information and their implications – part 1*; Extracted from the Journal of Creation-23 (2) 96 – 102, August 2009, https://creation.com/laws-of-information-1

USER-DEFINED SOFTWARE

Industrial DEFinition Methods, *IDEF Family of Methods, A Structured Approach to Enterprise Modeling & Analysis,* Knowledge Based Systems Inc. http://www.idef.com/

Jacobson, Ivar; et al., *Object-Oriented Software Engineering - A Use Case Driven Approach*, Addison-Wesley, 1992.

KANBANize, *The Ultimate Guide to Kanban Software Development*, https://kanbanize.com/kanban-resources/case-studies/kanban-for-software-development-teams/

Kennedy, John F., Presidential Library and Museum, Historical Speeches, Address to Joint Session of Congress, May 25, 1961, https://www.jfklibrary.org/learn/about-jfk/historic-speeches/address-to-joint-session-of-congress-may-25-1961

Larman, Craig, *Iterative and Incremental Development: A Brief History*, Computer, (June 2003) p36 (6): 47–56.)

Merriam-Webster, https://www.merriam-webster.com/dictionary/customer

My Account Course, https://www.myaccountingcourse.com/accounting-dictionary/law-of-diminishing-returns

National Institute of Standards and Technology, Information Technology Laboratory, Computer Security Resource Center, https://csrc.nist.gov/glossary?index=P, https://www.nist.gov

Scriven, Michael & Paul, Richard, Critical Thinking, Defined by the National Council for Excellence in Critical Thinking, 1987, A statement by Michael Scriven & Richard Paul, presented at the 8th Annual International Conference on Critical Thinking and Education Reform, Summer- 987.

Schwaber, Ken and Sutherland, Jeff, *The Scrum Guide™*, November 2017

Software Testing Help, Spiral Model – What Is SDLC Spiral Model? August 21, 2019, https://www.softwaretestinghelp.com/spiral-model-what-is-sdlc-spiral-model/

USER-DEFINED SOFTWARE

The Peak Performance Center,
http://thepeakperformancecenter.com/business/strategic-management/the-law-of-diminishing-returns/

Thakur, Dinesh, *Types of Software Maintenance*, ECOMPUTER NOTES,
http://ecomputernotes.com/software-engineering/types-of-software-maintenance

Unified Modeling Language, https://www.uml.org/

HOFF INDUSTRIES

HOFF INDUSTRIES

HOFF INDUSTRIES is a SERVICE-DISABLED VETERAN and WOMAN OWNED SMALL BUSINESS

Frederick Hoff the primary author of User-Defined Software brings together over 22 years of software development expertise. His experience began in the United States Air Force as a Division Chief for software testing. He possesses an elaborate background in computer capacity analysis through software development and program management. He conceptualized and developed the 4-D model, used it to deliver world class software in his Air Force career and subsequently developed the model presented in this document.

He holds an Air War College, Professional Military Education Certification. He also holds a Master Degree from Troy University.

The primary editor, Christopher Davidson, holds a Doctorate of Law Degree.

Contributor: LeAnn Davidson
Contributor/Illustrator: Amanda Svenby
Contributor: Maegan Hoff
Contributor: Carmine Vilardi

INDEX

www.ingramcontent.com/pod-product-compliance
Lightning Source LLC
Chambersburg PA
CBHW041429050326
40690CB00002B/474